40 Conversations
With the Prophet ﷺ
On Art & Creative Process

Compiled and Translated by

Dr. Ali Hussain

Foreword by

Chaplain Kamau Ayubbi

Published and Distributed by:
Copyright 2023
The Adhwaq Center for Spirituality, Culture and the Arts
ISBN: 9781737306153
Email: info@adhwaqcenter.org
Web: https://www.adhwaqcenter.org
Photo Credit: Mario La Pergola from Unsplash

Table of Contents

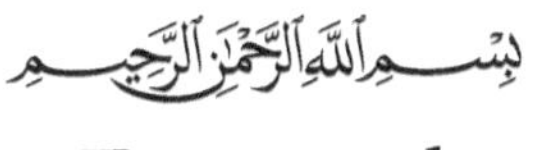

Foreword

Praise be to God who began creation with a Light from His Light and stirred it in an Ocean of Power as if dipping a paint brush, bundles of light in the Pigments of His Power, Mercy, Wisdom, Love and Justice. From that Muhammadan Light ﷺ he brought out the form and formless, He splashed from Eternal Realities until they settled and found their specific rhythms and patterns according to His Guiding Light.

With full Artistry, He allowed for a spectrum of Light to appear and give us shades, tones, and depths in creation. He granted creation consciousness and unconsciousness as a means of discovery, interpretation and illumination. Praise be to God who connected *idhn* (permission) to the *udhun* (ear), the physical symbol of hearing. It's in the quality of hearing from hearts and souls that we find 'permission' to 'hear' what God is telling us.

That's why the American tradition of Jazz, transmitted by hearts and souls of the African diaspora, was able to take Qur'anic tones and sensibilities into new art forms such as spirituals, the blues; to transmit a communication of meaning that is both structured and improvisational and produce inclusive cosmic sounds to the likes of Coltrane and other masters. The same can be said for any person inclined toward deeper meanings in the various genres of art as well as the craft of worshipful devotion to the Source of inward and outward beauty, aesthetics and meanings.

And The Choicest and Most Expanding Blessings upon Muhammad ﷺ the Praiseworthy, The Mercy who listened to and gazed upon the innovative beauty of loving expression via Quranic voice, poetry, instrumentation, dance and ecstatic improvisation. He ﷺ whose words hold the greatest ranges of meaning and interpretation to enrich the souls of humanity and bring light to the various arts and disciplines.

Dr. Ali Hussain is a student, teacher and artist with a mission of tracing the *idhn* (permission) inherent in creation. A movement to find traces of sacred meaning in the soul, spirit, art, culture and wherever else it may reveal itself. His association with and love for the Spiritual Masters of our time such as Habib Umar bin Hafiz and Shaykh Hisham Kabbani, as well as previous great saints and sages especially Shaykh al Akbar Ibn al-'Arabi, has opened in him the expansiveness of Islamic spirituality and Mercified Perception.

Combined with an artistic family, personal experiences and engagement with the arts, his shared thoughts make revenant connections through the threads of remembrance, perception, insight and Divine Attraction in the context of art and culture. This work is another ripened fruit of continuous attraction, effort and opening to witness the conversations between people, things and cultures as sacred memories of ancient conversations.

This publication gives us permission to witness these conversations and extract reminders from our souls to help us find our own sacred 'permission' to engage more freely in our creative potentials, in service to our individual and collective healing.

Chaplain Kamau Ayubbi

Detroit, Michigan
Tuesday September 12, 2023

Kamau Ayubbi is a native of California living in Detroit, Michigan, and has served as a hospital chaplain and workshop facilitator in various contexts of art, spirituality and healing for over sixteen years. His teachers include Shaykh Nazim Adil al-Haqqani and Shaykh Hisham Kabbani who have affirmed his upbringing in various arts, cultural contexts of his diverse spiritual and cultural roots. He has a degree in visual arts and interned in holistic health studies. He is also the founder of heavenlytek.com vending 'soulful wares for soul care'.

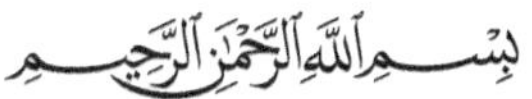

Introduction

Al-Bayhaqi narrates that the Prophet ﷺ said: "Whoever preserves for my community forty *hadiths* [conversations, teachings] that benefit them in their religion. They will be resurrected among the scholars on the Day of Judgment."

I would like this hadith to guide this introduction. Beginning with the word *hadith* that I have intentionally translated as 'conversation' in the title of the book, opting for a more intimate choice than 'sayings' or 'teachings' as is often used by translators.

The word *hadith* is a rich homonym in Arabic, meaning there are at least two Arabic variations that are pronounced exactly the same, with drastically different meanings. The first of these we have already mentioned, 'conversation', while the second is 'recent' or 'new'.

Thus, God describes remembrance in the Qur'an as *dhikr muhdath*, or a recent arrival. The Prophet ﷺ beautifully describes rain as *hadith 'ahd bi-rabbih* (a recent arrival from its

Lord), as a response to a companion who asks why the Prophet ﷺ exposed his head and body to rainfall.

I intend to capture both these meanings of *hadith* in this book. Many of the statements mentioned between these two covers can be found in countless compendiums of prophetic narrations, in both Arabic and English.

I pray and hope to present them anew by regarding them, first and foremost, as intimate conversations with the Prophet ﷺ and, secondly, to excavate from them meanings for a new audience, time and space.

It should not be lost on anyone in the Muslim community, especially artists, that Muslim creatives are not fully appreciated in the West by their community, neither spiritually, financially nor institutionally.

Art is often perceived as frivolous entertainment that should be approached as a hobby in favor of more 'serious' vocations that bring six-digit salaries and financial stability in a world that our scripture ironically reminds constantly is a fleeting apparition.

Aside from my intention for Divine Pleasure, I specifically compiled, translated and offered my own commentary in this book as a gift for my own community of Muslim artists. I present this not only as a token of meaningful content, but more importantly as a statement that we, Muslim artists, matter.

As the storytellers in our community, those who carry the burden of marking memories and making memoirs, we deserve to have sacred discourses written specifically with us in mind. It is not an arrogant expectation, but rather irrigating a future of a community, forgotten in body, yet engraved in the spirit of words, colors and sounds.

The Muslim community is unfortunately oblivious about this crucial role of art as a homily for lost homes and civilizations. Nevertheless, we Muslim artists are not. We recognize the gravity of this moment in our age and the inevitable looming presence of our graves.

With this in mind, I present you with this book, *40 Conversations with the Prophet ﷺ: On Art and the Creative Process*. The organization of this work is very simple. It consists of four chapters, the first of which focuses on key verses from the Qur'an that are tethered to art and the creative process.

The second is the book's highlight of 40 conversations from the hadith collection, while the third focuses on teachings from the 12th century Andalusian mystic Ibn al-'Arabi. As some might recount from my previous publication, *A Nostalgic Remembrance: Sufism and the Breath of Creativity*, Ibn al-'Arabi is my spiritual guide in appreciating the sacred dimensions of the creative process.

It is also his own collection of 40 hadiths, titled *Mishkat al-Anwar* (The Niche of Lights), that inspired the content and structure of this book. Therefore, not only does *al-shaykh al-akbar* (The Greatest Master) appear in the commentary of all the sections of the book, but I have also decided to dedicate an entire section to his teachings, based on my conviction of their indispensable benefit to Muslim – and non-Muslim – artists.

The fourth and last section focuses on stories and statements by other Muslim scholars and saints throughout history, even some contemporary figures. The straightforward organization also hearkens to a catered format that I have used in my previous book, *A Nostalgic Remembrance*.

Specifically, my choice to couple verses from the Qur'an and hadiths with statements by non-Muslim artists returns in this book. As I mentioned in *A Nostalgic Remembrance*, my objective is to explicitly liberate the Qur'an and prophetic teachings from the strict theological and legalistic prison wherein they have been placed and to instead view them through a contemporary, relevant and revenant prism.

In this way, Sir Michael Caine, Nina Simone, Miles Davis and Toni Morrison grace us in the following pages to offer a contemporary interpretation of Islam. But more than that, also as is my objective in *A Nostalgic Remembrance*, I pray and hope that this book can be a meaningful introduction of – more than 'to' – Islam in the West.

I reiterate my conviction that the veracity of a faith tradition lies in its ability to meet people where they are, without any expectation of conversion or reversion. Can Islam converse with and revere people in their different contexts? I believe it can, and this is my attempt in facilitating such a meeting.

It is precisely because I believe that culture, as a collective of individual imaginations, is a sacred translation of scripture and spiritual traditions that I have focused on the creative process, art and popular culture in both this book and *A Nostalgic Remembrance*. It is from this vantage point also that I think these two projects complete one another.

At the risk of pedantry and arrogance, I pray that the relationship between *40 Conversations* and *A Nostalgic Remembrance* intimates the marriage between Ibn al-'Arabi's *Bezels of Wisdom* and *The Meccan Openings*; the former of which summarizes the latter in a condensed form.

Aside from the coupling of scripture or hadith with statements by contemporary artists, the format of each section also includes my own short commentary on each pair of teachings. These torrents were poetic reflections disguised as prose. While I tried my best to leave them simple, like falling leaves they naturally fluctuated between explanations or explorations.

I then conclude each commentary with a few prompts for you, the artist, with which to engage as you wish in the empty space at the bottom of the page. It is here that *40 Conversations* emerges as a possible diary for you to converse in word, color or any other medium with the Qur'an, the Prophet ﷺ or the scholars and saints from our tradition.

One last word on format, specifically pertaining to references and resources. As readers of *A Nostalgic Remembrance* are well aware, I dislike the inclusion of references as a means of detering readers from perceiving my books as academic or religious texts and instead to approach them as works of art about art.

While I still adhere to this same principle, I also acknowledge that this book is somewhat different, since it is specifically a collection of references from scripture and prophetic hadiths. With this in mind, I have kept the citations to a minimum, only in the first two sections.

Thus, you can find the chapter and verse number for each of the Qur'anic references in the first section. As for the second, I have included the *musnad* (biographical) or *musannaf* (topical) compendium in which the specific hadith can be found.

There are a few exceptions to this, including a few instances of Hadith Qudsi – where the Prophet ﷺ directly quotes God - that despite their doubtful authenticity according to *naql* (transmitted sources) are nevertheless authenticated according to *kashf* (unveiling), as Ibn al-'Arabi and other Muslim saints emphasize.

It is worthwhile mentioning that the content of the references in this book is catered less so for us Muslim artists to validate our craft and passion for others in the community and more so for us to grow in our own journey with God, through our creative work.

I am sure many of us are physically and spiritually tired of the need to explain to other Muslims that enjoying musical instruments, portrait painting, singing Western music other than *nasheed* or sculpture does not render us hell bound. I would go further and say that even engaging in these debates and conversations is actually harmful for us as artists.

Let us be unequivocal about this: we have no responsibility towards our religious community, neither as people, institutions, discourses or leaders, to explain or validate our inner calling and passion. As I mentioned above, the Muslim community – despite its unawareness – actually needs Muslim artists to tell its story, not the other way around.

Many of the people – and perhaps even institutions or discourses – that oppose our creative journeys now, no matter how dear and near to us, might not be here in 30 years to answer for the regret we will feel for not pursuing and cultivating our God-given gifts and talents.

And so, while some of the references in this book directly speak about the arts, others are less direct and meant to help artists take ownership of their faith and see themselves comfortably and confidently as its custodians, of no less importance than the theologian and legal-scholar.

I pray and hope that this work is accepted by God and the Prophet ﷺ and that, per the reward mentioned by the Prophet ﷺ in the 'conversation' with which I started this introduction, that this book is a means for both me and chaplain Kamau Ayubbi, who wrote the exquisite foreword, to be resurrected with those scholars of word, color and sound known as artists on the Day of Judgment.

Let us keep creating with Divine Grace and Beauty!

Ali Hussain

Fenton, MI
Monday September 11, 2023

Dr. Ali Hussain is a musician and poet. He has a doctoral degree in Sufism from the University of Michigan, Department of Middle Eastern Studies. In 2018, he founded The Adhwaq Center of Spirituality, Culture, and the Arts; an endeavor focused on spirituality and creativity in contemporary culture.

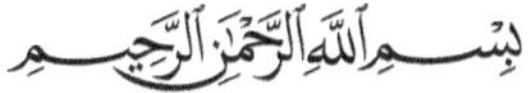

Chapter One: *The Qur'an*

"This is the dye of God. And whose dye is more beautiful than God's and we are worshipping Him."
(2:138)

———

"This is God's universe and he is the master gardener of all. If we were to eliminate all colors in his garden, then what would be a rainbow with only one color? Or a garden with only one kind of flower? Why would the Creator create a vast assortment of plants, ethnicities, and animals, if only one beast or seed is to dominate all of existence?"
- Suzy Kassem

God exalts a few things in the Qur'an. Among these, He has chosen to mention His Dye, which many exegetes interpret as Islam.

But He has mentioned that elsewhere. Here, He is specifically focusing on dye as a precursor to worship. As the author Suzy Kassem mentions, everything in the universe reveals a color and hue specifically chosen by God.

For the artist, it is not simply a matter of appreciating and deciphering this kaleidoscope of artistry in the universe around us, but also reflecting on our inner palette. What are our inherent colors? Why has God made us inclined to particular hues and not others?

More importantly, how do our colors of choice reflect, refract and mirror our dispositions? Is our anger, empathy, longing, patience or gratitude symbolized by particular hues?

"You have no hand in the affair."
(3:128)

"When Jack Lemmon started acting in film, after a long
career in theater, the director was trying to help him bring
down his energy in front of the camera. 'Do less Jack', the
director kept repeating. 'If I do any less, I'll do nothing',
replied Jack. 'That's it Jack, do nothing!' said the director."
-    Sir Michael Caine

The artist is constantly pushed to the abyss of their own self, to come to terms with the fact that the best work they can make is that which is channeled, not forced, through them.

Jack Lemmon experienced that firsthand, not only in presence of his director, but more importantly the hidden saint of the craft, the instrument known as the camera.

The word camera comes from the Arabic *qamaria*, which means a small window. It is also phonetically related to two names of God: *al-Qarib* (the near) and *al-Raqib* (Watchful), both of which aptly describe the camera.

Like all instruments of art, the camera is the wind behind the movement of its craft, yet it is never shown gratitude for the work it helps produce. Rather, it is the director, producer and

3

actors who are applauded. In this way, the instrument teaches the artist how to be selfless as instruments themselves in the Hand of the Divine Artist.

We call those instruments in the Hand of God prophets and saints. Meanwhile, art is the Divine Gift granted to help human beings become channels of beauty as masters and saints of their own craft. What is your instrument and how does it teach you selflessness and 'being nothing'?

"Tell stories that they might reflect."
(7:176)

———

"Tell your story. This is the one thing an oppressor cannot
take away from you, your story"
\-   Toni Morrison

Among the many commands in the Qur'an, His final testament to humanity, God orders us to tell stories. What is at stake in telling or forsaking our stories?

We do not simply tell stories to pass time, but rather to form a sacred sense of time that makes sense in the grand scheme of our existence. We wish to perceive our life as meaningful in the larger narrative of the universe.

Since time immemorial, we have told stories. What is common among all these tales is the presence of a protagonist hero with weaknesses and strengths and an antagonist villain who exploits these shortcomings to try and prevent the hero from their triumph.

As the late Toni Morrison shows, the need to tell stories is one of survival. However, it is not only to commemorate the memories of the oppressed that we write narratives, but also to discover our own inner heroes and villains, all of whom linger in amorphous darkness and ambivalence inside our souls until we coax and draw them out with pen and ink in hand.

Think of the stories you have written or wish to write: who or what are your inner heroes and villains? What are the shortcomings and strengths of your protagonist and how can they overcome the connivance of your own antagonist?

"You did not throw, when you threw, but God threw."
(8:17)

———

"Art is a collaboration between God and the artist, and the
less the artist does the better."
-    Andre Gide

Returning to the importance of doing and being nothing
above, this manifests in the most detailed minutiae of your
craft.

We have to consciously suspend every brush, letter and note
stroke upward, to heavens. We seek more to hear God breathe
art through us, as we listen attentively, than the other way
around.

Like repentance, whence a person will forget their sin when it
is fully forgiven, so can an artist also get whatever they give in
their craft entirely of themselves for God.

In this way, the creative process may be thought of as one of
repentance, of taking oneself into account through a medium
of beauty.

Undoubtedly, art is a mirror for the artist that makes us face ourselves, our inner demons and angels. This culminates in a work which the audience interprets on its own terms but that can have an entirely different power and meaning for the artist themselves.

However, according to the sincerity of the artist's repentance so can the audience also experience a genuine taste of their art. What has been the experience of repentance in your craft?

These words in the verse are voiced by Mary the mother of Jesus, peace be upon them. She sought a higher order of what we have spoken about so far: to be nothing and produce the work of art that had been delegated to her, Jesus, with little human effort.

The Chinese photographer Song Dong eloquently capitulates this prayer of Mary with his explanation of the two deaths in Chinese culture: demise through forgetfulness.

For many Sufi masters like Ibn al-'Arabi, the two deaths are that of the ego followed by the body. But each of these deaths is received by God as an exchange, after which the human being is gifted a new lease on life.

Mary's prayer and Song Dong's statement make us as artists come face to face with our own inevitable exchange with God, the need to die twice in order to be resurrected also two times in some way or another.

What are you, as an artist, willing to forego, forget or be forgotten as in order to receive? Do we desire to be lost within the words, colors or sounds we produce? If so, how do we hope to be resurrected?

**"God is the Light of the heavens and earth. The example
of His Light is like a niche within which resides a lamp.
The lamp is in glass. The glass is like a glowing star
ignited from a blessed tree, neither easterly nor westerly.
Its oil ignites without being touched by fire. Light upon
light, and God guides to His Light whomever He wills.
These parables God gives to people and He knows all
things."
(24:35)**

———

"My work is about your seeing. There is a rich tradition in
painting of work about light, but it is not light — it is the
record of seeing. My material is light, and it is responsive to
your seeing."
-    James Turrell

The relationship between light and matter is remarkable. The
meeting of all hues in matter yields the color black, whereas
their absence results in white. Meanwhile, in light the opposite
is true. The addition of all colors yield white while their absence
produces black light.

As the Qur'anic verse shows, light participates in the meeting
of east and west, which symbolize here all senses of
oppositions. Ultimately, as in the diagram of Yin and Yang,
light and darkness cooperate to meet in a neutral zone that Ibn
al-ʿArabi would call *maqam al-la maqam* (station of no-station).

Thenceforth, the artist James Turrell brings our attention to the importance of perception in augmenting the power of light. This is not only important in art, but Turrell is alluding in his work to the role of perception in life and how it affects our reception of truth and reality.

How do both senses of light (subtlety and glow) appear in your craft? Might there be light in music? How do light and darkness help you as an artist find the meeting between east and west in your work?

"Each has come to know their prayer and praise."
(24:41)

———

"Good art is a form of prayer. It's a way to say what is not
sayable."
-      Frederick Busch

Whereas humans have five designated times for prayer, all
other beings are continuously praising God. However, our
species is also capable of continuous prayer, as the Qur'an
mentions.

But what does this continuous prayer look like? It cannot be a
physical ritual like the five designated prayers since those have
already been ordained.

Rather, this continuous prayer has to be something that we
involuntarily do, that we inhale and exhale as seamlessly as our
breaths.

It must also be a movement that we can never tire of. Rather,
we incessantly seek and desire it, even after engaging in it for
hours to no end.

This private prayer is nothing but our passion and calling. It is the medium through which we are meant to tell the story that God wants to unfold through us during our lifetime on this earth.

What is your private prayer? Think of the five ritual prayers, their pillars and requirements (ablution, purity) how do you dance with all of that in your own craft and passion as an artist?

"Work oh people of David in gratitude. For indeed, very few people are grateful."
(34:13)

———

"The essence of all beautiful art, all great art, is gratitude."
- Frederick Nietzsche

The association between *shukr* (gratitude) in this verse and the prophet David is crucial because he is known in both the Judeo-Christian and Islamic traditions as the great musician.

The Prophet ﷺ regularly praised Abu Musa al-Ashari for his beautiful recitation of the Qur'an by telling him: "You have been gifted a reed-flute from those given to the family of David."

Muslim saints like Abdul Aziz al-Dabbagh also emphasize that the path of sainthood is that of *shukr* (gratitude) not *zuhd* (asceticism). In turn, as Nietzsche also says, the path of the artist and saint are one.

They are the same because both the artist and saint, as we have mentioned above, are in the business of doing and being nothing. Gratitude completes this vision by helping us recognize the immensity of Divine Grace.

Whereas *zuhd* (asceticism) entails struggling to achieve something, *shukr* (gratitude) is all about being nothing yet blessed to receive and channel everything.

How does asceticism and gratitude find its way to your craft? Which path do you find yourself inclined to take? What are you grateful for? How do you think you can be even more grateful?

"Remind, for indeed memory benefits the believers."
(51:55)

———

"Memory is a great artist. For every man and for every
woman it makes the recollection of his or her life a work of
art and an unfaithful record."
-    Andre Maurois

This verse is almost always mistranslated as: "Remind, for
indeed reminding benefits the believers." However, *dhikra*, the
word used in the Qur'an, does not mean 'reminding' rather
memory.

It is precisely the connection between *dhikr* (remembrance) and
dhikra (memory) that makes this verse and act of worship so
relevant and revenant today. As the Qur'anic story of Moses
shows, our relationship with God is not meant to divorce us
from the messiness of our lives, but enforce its sacredness.

When Moses meets God for the first time at the burning bush,
God recounts to him his entire life story, informing Moses that
He was with him every step of the way, even though he
inadvertently killed one of Pharaoh's soldiers.

Reiterating Andre Maurois' sentiment, God also wanted Moses to perceive the beautiful canvas that He had painted of and for him throughout all his trials and tribulations.

Let our art be not only our private prayer, but our *dhikr* (remembrance) as well. What Divine Names manifest to you during your solemn remembrance? What memories keep resurfacing at the shore of your work?

"Those who are continuously in prayer."
(70:23)

———

"If art is only a full-time job for you, then please, do not
waste your time and that of the craft. When I go home after a
long day at the set, I cannot leave my characters behind. They
come home with me."
-     Sir Michael Caine

We come to the verse mentioned above and the need to be
continuously in prayer, which we mentioned is our inner
calling, passion and craft.

Sir Michael Caine gives us another insight into what this
continuous prayer can and should look like. Although each of
us as artists might not be physically practicing our art every
moment of our lives, it should nevertheless never escape our
heart and mind.

If after practicing my Oud for 3 hours I feel relieved to part
ways with my instrument, that is a bad sign. If on the other
hand, I feel longing to pick it up again and play as soon as I put
it away, that is a sign of a healthy passion. This is how I know
this IS my passion.

As many Oud teachers have explained, the serious student

engages with their craft for approximately 6 hours daily, 3 of which are only physical practice. The rest include attentive listening, reading and thinking about the instrument.

How do you try to continuously be in prayer in your craft? Other than your physical practice, what habits have you developed to maintain a creative flow?

"As for the bounty of your Lord, then proclaim."
(93:10)

———

"You can't use up creativity. The more you use, the more you
have."
- Maya Angelou

Artists should never be afraid of sharing their gift with the
world nor should they reject praise. I will explain: to reject
praise and insist that you are not very good at what you do is
assuming that you are the sole creator of your art.

However, in reality, the artist is a channel for Divine Creativity.
It is true, you have been elected by God to express and
manifest His Beauty. You were chosen not due to any merit,
but a wisdom and disposition in you that only He knows about.

It is not our responsibility to try and explain this election, only
to fulfill its obligation and responsibility. The reverence due to
this grant is that we manifest it, whereas hiding or neglecting it
under the false pretenses of piety and humbleness is actually
the epitome of ingratitude.

The true sense of humility for the artist comes in
acknowledging our singular ability: the craft, the calling and art.

We humble ourselves by developing the conviction in what is our actual strength, thereby admitting the possibility of ineptitude in practically everything else, and to be fine with that.

What sense of responsibility do you feel towards your craft and talent given by God? So far, how have you detected false senses of piety and humbleness in your work?

Chapter Two: *40 Conversations*

Al-Manawi narrates that Aisha said: "The prophet ﷺ used to speak with us and us with him. Then, when prayer time came, he went to pray as if he did not know us nor us him."

————

"He would be talking with us, then if a scene presents itself to him to be photographed, he will forget everything and just focus on his lens and the scene."
-    Wife of photographer Richard Misrach

The harmony here between the attentiveness that the Prophet ﷺ gave to the ritual prayer and photographer Richard Misrach gives to his private prayer, photography, is uncanny.

I am a firm believer that connections and similarities such as this one reveal themselves to whoever is looking, and I am constantly seeking them.

As I explained in my book, *A Nostalgic Remembrance: Sufism and the Breath of Creativity*, creativity and the mystical experience are mirrored movements. In both instances, we try to 'make connections where none seem possible or exist' and 'translate the ineffable into the tangible.'

But what do we exactly do with this mirroring between the life of the Prophet ﷺ and Richard Misrach, where even the narrators in both instances are of the same archetype: their wives?

We acknowledge the sacredness of the craft as our prayer. We pay attention to our creative inspiration as it arrives and turn ourselves to it completely. Those are the moments that heaven is calling us and we have to hearken. Have you experienced such moments of call and hearken from a creative inspiration before?

Abu Dawud narrates that the Prophet ﷺ said: "The holy spirit is with Hassan so long as he defends the Messenger ﷺ."

———

"The Romans and Greeks did not believe poets were geniuses but that they had a genius, a muse that inspired you to write poetry and art."
-      Elizabeth Gilbert

It is important to understand that defending the prophet ﷺ in this context is not of a specific form. Since every manifestation of beauty alludes to God's Beauty in some way, it is also an affirmation of his message ﷺ.

Taking this into consideration, the Prophet ﷺ affirms here the sacred movement of art and the creative process. He confirms that the source of creativity and poetry is not the human mind or psyche, but the holy spirit, an angelic presence that supports and inspires the artist.

What this ultimately means also is that creativity comes from the same source as revelation. This is confirmed in another hadith where he ﷺ says: "The righteous vision is one tenth of prophethood."

And so, our responsibility as artists emerges in acknowledging the sanctity and sacrality of our calling. Despite all modernist attempts, mostly within our Muslim community, to dismiss art as frivolous entertainment, both the Prophet ﷺ and Elizabeth Gilbert remind us that there is a deeper spiritual reality to the work we produce.

How has the holy spirit and muse made its presence known to you during your creative process?

Abu Dawud narrates that the Prophet ﷺ said: "Indeed, some poetry is wisdom."

"Poetry is when an emotion has found its thought and the thought has found words."
-    Robert Frost

Many Muslims misinterpret verses like: "He is not a poet nor does it befit him" or "poets are followed by those who are astray" to be a disparagement of poetry. However, as Ibn al-'Arabi explains, revelation is not poetry because the former contains laws that have to be explained in clear prose.

On the other hand, poetry is the exclusive domain of the ambiguous and ambivalent, more fit for spiritual realities. In turn, practically every Muslim saint throughout history has written poetry, the most celebrated among which is Mevlana Rumi's compendium *The Mathnavi*, which was known as the 'Qur'an in Persian'.

The word that the Prophet ﷺ uses here to associate with poetry, *hikma* (wisdom) is etymologically tethered to another term, *hukm* (ruling); a connection that Ibn al-'Arabi emphasizes in his writings.

But what ruling exactly? The intricate affairs of wisdom that govern this universe. In other words, poetry is an expression of the Divine Creative Process. Frost alludes to this by highlighting that poetry has the power to express the inexpressible.

How does poetry and poiesis appear in your craft? What wisdom do you constantly hope to manifest through your work?

Ahmad narrates that Umar entered the mosque while Abyssinians were dancing with their spears and tried to stop them with pebbles. The Prophet ﷺ told him: "Let them be Umar, they are the sons of Arfida."

———

"The great artists of the past were aware that human life is full of chaos and suffering. But they had a remedy for this. And the name of that remedy was 'beauty'. The beautiful work of art brings consolation in sorrow and affirmation in joy. It shows human life to be worthwhile."
 -   Roger Scruton

The Prophet's ﷺ response to Umar in this incident needs to be explained. He mentions the lineage of the Abyssinians as descendants of Arfida to emphasize that this is the way they express joy and happiness, by dancing with their spears and drumming.

Like the 'great artists of the past' that Scruton mentions, the Abyssinians were not only expressing their own joy of being in the presence of the Divine Viceroy but also hoping to spread that joy to others.

More importantly, by acknowledging and affirming them, the Prophet ﷺ emphasizes his role as a divinely ordained artist as well. He had been sent by God as a giver of glad tidings and joy, which he in turn encouraged the companions to do as well: "Give glad tidings and do not turn people away."

The power of this prophetic affirmation stands as a consolation, to use Scruton's expression, for all artists today. This is especially true for Muslim artists whose calling and talent are unfortunately rarely acknowledged by their community.

What are some ways you try to consciously manifest joy through your work?

Abu Dawud narrates the Prophet ﷺ said: "They are not from us those who do not melodiously recite the Qur'an."

———

"Music is the melody whose text is the world."
- Arthur Schopenhauer

This hadith stands as the great proponent of music and musicality in Islam, alongside the prophetic praise for poetry and drawing, which we will see later in this chapter.

By setting melody as a boundary for belonging to the community, the Prophet ﷺ establishes musicality as an obligation in our engagement with scripture. But what does that exactly mean?

It entails that melody is not simply ornament or decoration, but a necessary component to unlocking the meanings of God's Words. The Qur'an simply cannot be understood without melody.

This is foundational in the art of Qur'an recitation in Egypt, especially during the first half of the 20th century where reciters relied upon the modalities of Arabic music, *maqamat*, to emotionally convey and embody meanings of Qur'anic verses.

Melody and its various organs: pitch, modulation and tonal intervals can viscerally convey meaning much more poignantly than can a rational understanding of the Arabic language.

32

What ulterior methods do you use in your craft to convey meaning to your audience in your work? Can an artist offload meaning from their words to the texture of paper, canvas or silence between notes?

Ahmad narrates that the Prophet ﷺ said: "Beautify the Qur'an with your voices."

"The human voice was the first instrument and remains the most powerful and effective method of musical creation and emotional transference."
-    Deke Sharon

This hadith reiterates the emphasis on musicality in Qur'an recitation from the previous page, with the addition that the human voice emerges as a catalyst that can beautify scripture.

The power of this relationship between human voice and revelation is that the beauty of Divine Speech depends on human sound in order to fully manifest.

This proves that the human voice does not merely ornament the Qur'an but participates in the unfolding of its meanings. Deke Sharon also reiterates what Ibn al-'Arabi states, that the first scripture was pure music.

More than that, he presents music as the ancestor of spoken language since sustained sound when disconnected at particular places and changed in pitch and intonation results in speech.

More importantly, the emphasis on the human voice as the primordial device problematizes any attempt to dismiss other musical instruments. Especially since our vocal organ is considered both a wind and string instrument.

How do you beautify your art? If your craft does not fall under the auditory arts, does voice and music appear in some other way in your work?

Ahmad narrates that the Prophet ﷺ said: "God listens more attentively to the reciter with a beautiful voice than one of you does to their instrument."

———

"The human voice is the most beautiful instrument of all, the most moving... And even the greatest virtuoso in the world will never be able to give you even a fraction of the emotion that a beautiful voice can give you. That is our share of the divine."
-   Anna Gavalda

In the Qur'an, the imperative conjugation of *sami'a*, to hear, is never used. Rather, it is always the more intensive morphological form of *istami'* that is prevalent, which translates to 'listen attentively'.

This requires a silencing of all other noises whilst listening to the Divine Voice. In one particular verse, God adds another dimension to this audition: "If the Qur'an is recited, then listen to it attentively and *ansitu* [be silent] that you may receive mercy." (7:204)

If *istima'* is attentive listening in body, then *insat* maybe thought of as attentive listening in soul and spirit. However, in this hadith, neither *insat* nor *istima'* is used, rather the more intimate expression *ashaddu udhunan* (lit. stronger in ear) is utilized.

Incidentally, a similar wording can be found to describe the Prophet ﷺ in the Qur'an, when his tribe of Quraysh describe him ﷺ as 'an ear', due to his deep listening to their complains and burdens.

How does deep listening emerge in your work? How can we listen to colors and words? We may be able to give voice to the latter, but can we allow hues to speak and peak through mediums other than our sight and vision?

Ahmad narrates that Ibn Mas'ud said that the Prophet ﷺ drew a square in the sand with a line inside this square. He then drew small lines around this line inside the square and another line outside the square. He asked: "Do you know what this is?" They said: "God and His Messenger know best". He said: "This square is the human being. These small lines are accidents that try to devour him at every turn. As for the square, it is death and the line extending outside the square, that is his hopes and desires."

———

"Abstraction allows man to see with his mind what he cannot see physically with his eyes.... Abstract art enables the artist to perceive beyond the tangible, to extract the infinite out of the finite. It is the emancipation of the mind. It is an exploration into unknown areas."
-      Arshile Gorky

So much can and should be said about this incredible hadith.

It is important to note that everything the Prophet ﷺ said is revelation, as God affirms in the Qur'an: "He does not utter from whim, rather it is a sent revelation" (53:3).

This sanctity and sacrality of the Prophetic speech necessarily extends to the medium through which he ﷺ expressed these Divine Sparks. In other words, just as the Arabic language is sacred, so is the medium of abstract art that he ﷺ used here to express this beautiful drawing depicting the fragility of human life.

Like many hadiths so far, this incident from the life of the Prophet ﷺ further sanctifies the mission of the artist: as a receiver and conveyer of Divine Inspiration and what is beyond the tangible, as Arshile Gorky states.

How does abstraction emerge in your art? And what are the different ways in which Divine Inspiration makes itself known to you in your craft during the different stages of your work?

Bukhari narrates that the Prophet ﷺ told Abu Musa al-Ash'ari: "You have been gifted a reed-flute from those given to the people of David."

———

"The flute is the true magical rod that changes all it touches in the inward world; an enchanter's wand at which the secret depths of the soul open."
-      Jean Paul

Returning to the importance of musicality in Qur'an recitation. By comparing the beauty of human voice, specifically that of the companion Abu Musa al-Ashari, the Prophet ﷺ is also indirectly elevating the status of musical instruments.

While it is true that the 'reed-flutes of the people of David' is a reference to the beauty of this prophet's and his people's voices, it further establishes the sanctity of musical instruments as imagery for the power of prophetic speech and its ability to convey Divine Revelation.

In other words, the Prophet ﷺ would not have used this expression to praise the voice of his companion in recitation of the Qur'an if musical instruments were forbidden or satanic. In some narrations, upon hearing this praise, al-Ashari remarks: "If I had known that you were listening, I would have beautified it even more for you."

Beyond this, this hadith also revisits the intimate relationship between melody and scripture. God's Words hearken for melody and human voice to bring out their meanings in regal beauty.

Do you ever feel a certain prophetic inheritance manifesting through your work? How would you channel the 'reed-flute of the people of David' through the written or visual arts?

Bukhari narrates that Gabriel asked the Prophet ﷺ: "Tell me about *ihsan* [perfective beauty]" He ﷺ said: "That you worship God as though you see Him, for if you do not perceive Him, He sees you."

———

"Imagination is the beginning of creation. You imagine what you desire, you will what you imagine, and at last, you create what you will."
-   George Bernard Shaw

Ibn al-'Arabi states that this hadith is proof that we must imagine God whilst worshipping Him. He discusses this in relation to imagination, an excerpt that we will revisit in later sections.

But it is actually the context of this hadith that is equally important. For it is not a coincidence that the archangel Gabriel, the holy spirit, is the catalyst for this conversation with the Prophet ﷺ in this hadith.

Not only does he support poets like Hassan, as we saw in a previous hadith, but it is also Gabriel who casts the Word of God Jesus to Mary. Christ, as Ibn al-'Arabi states, has an imaginal body; a mixture between the physical water of Mary and spiritual reality of Gabriel.

In turn, this image of God that we bring into our imagination during worship is the foundation for intimacy in our rituals. As Bernard Shaw highlights, such an imaginal exercise has tremendous consequences on our will and actions in the physical world.

Ibn al-ʿArabi would agree, since he states that the physical world is rooted in the spiritual. Do you imagine God often in your art? Do you hear Him guiding you in your craft and work? If so, how and what does He say to you?

Al-Darimi narrates that the Prophet ﷺ said: "I saw my Lord in the most beautiful form."

"Beauty is eternity gazing at itself in a mirror."
-   Khalil Gibran

And here we continue with our conversation from the previous hadith, on the importance of imagining God during worship. The Prophet ﷺ himself shares that He saw God in a beautiful form.

Khalil Gibran reveals a subtlety behind this vision: that any beauty we see in God or the world is ultimately a reflection of our own inner beauty. As we will see in a later hadith, this is confirmed by the Divine statement: "I am at My Servant's opinion of Me. So let them think of Me well."

But in the case of the Prophet ﷺ himself, this point is particularly vivid, since as Ibn al-'Arabi and many other saints emphasize, his reality and light ﷺ is the very fabric from which God created the universe.

In this way, *al-haqiqa al-muhammadiyya* (Muhammadan Reality) and *al-nur al-muhammadi* (Muhammadan Light) are Islam's reconceptualization of *logos*. And so, the Prophet ﷺ perceived God through the perfection of his own form.

Of course, what is also moving in this hadith is the beauty of images and forms and their role in building our relationship with God. In other words, beauty in form is melody for our vision.

What form(s) might God take in your work when He speaks to you? Do these images have any particular significance in your memories or memoirs?

Abu Dawud narrates that the Prophet ﷺ said: "Indeed, time has curved in its original form on the day that God created the heavens and earth."

———

"Time is an illusion. Time only exists when we think about the past and the future. Time doesn't exist in the present here and now."
-   Marina Abramovic

It is remarkable that among all that the Prophet ﷺ says during the final sermon of his first and only pilgrimage, this statement barely receives any attention. This singular expression that consecrates our sufferings and redemptions with a heavenly purpose is rarely acknowledged.

Saints like Ibn al-'Arabi deduce from this statement that time is indeed cyclical. We move through the moments of our lives just as we would through space, in a *mi'raj* (curved ascension).

This means that our life is a collage of repeated patterns, events and interactions with people who despite their unique appearances are in fact recurrent archetypes sent to teach us a lesson about ourselves.

Herein comes the poignant statement by Marina Abramovic that time is an illusion. Ibn al-'Arabi agrees as he describes time as a mirage of procession and sequence, resulting from the finite Divine Theopanies permeating the finite container of the universe. However, much like imagined borders between nation states, the effect of this illusion is very much felt and real.

Do you find cyclical time appearing in your work? Have you ever experienced déjà vu in your art? Does the smell of dye or ink ever remind you of what seems like a past life?

Ahmad narrates that the Prophet ﷺ said: "The entire earth has been ordained as a *masjid* for me."

———

"Behind the cotton wool is hidden a pattern; that we—I mean all human beings—are connected with this; that the whole world is a work of art; that we are parts of the work of art. Hamlet or a Beethoven quartet is the truth about this vast mass that we call the world."
- Virginia Woolf

So much can be deduced from this hadith. We remember the first excerpt in this section about attentiveness to prayer and Richard Misrach's obliviousness to his surroundings when a scene presents itself to be photographed.

Here, the Prophet ﷺ shows that every atom of this universe is a possibility for prayer. It is important to note that the word *masjid* linguistically does not refer to a building, but the actual site of prostration, which does not have to be a mosque.

But we can also extend the notion of *sujud* (prostration), since as the Prophet said: "The person is closest to his Lord during prostration" (Abu Dawud) and prayer has been described by many scholars and saints as the 'ascension of the believer'.

We deduce from all of this that every atom in this universe is an opportunity for a prostration and ascension to God. Virginia Woolf, despite being a self-professed agnostic, reveals her own *masjid* in the cotton fields.

She experiences a raw sense of *tawhid* (oneness) through *tashbih*, or the intimate presence of Divinity in the world. How would you describe your workshop, studio or writing desk as your *masjid*? What does prostration look like in your craft and art?

Bukhari narrates that A'isha said two girls were singing in her house while the Prophet ﷺ laid on his side facing away from them. When Abu Bakr entered, he scolded the girls and said: "The flute of the devil in the house of the Prophet?" The Prophet ﷺ told him: "Let them be."

———

"A child sings before it speaks, dances almost before it walks. Music is in our hearts from the beginning."
- Pamela Brown

We follow the *sunna* (custom) of the Prophet ﷺ and echo this sentiment by telling our community: "Let us be!" But we also acknowledge that this does not absolve the community, and ourselves as its members, of the responsibility to sustain art and artists in our midst.

If the Muslim community, particularly in the West, does not invest in its artists as it does in religious scholars, the only memories and memoirs that will remain of it are dry legal edicts bereft of the fragility of human weakness.

Stories are history told in the first person. They problematize the universal by particularizing it. They show, as Mevlana Rumi says in the Mathnavi, that "beyond belief and unbelief there is a field", where he and other saints hope to meet us when we are ready.

This is precisely where the Prophet ﷺ wanted Abu Bakr to meet him ﷺ, as he and his wife Aisha listened to the girls' singing.

This is also where he ﷺ is asking our community to meet him and us, Muslim artists, at a creative space beyond right and wrong where our complexities and burdens can breathe and speak.

How do you let your art be? What are you strategies to step back and allow a work to breathe through you, as opposed to you breathing it into being?

Al-Tabarani narrates the Prophet ﷺ said: "God loves that when one of you does something that they perfect it."

____

"Art is choosing to do something skillfully, caring about the details, bringing all of yourself to make the finest work you can. It is beyond ego, vanity, self-glorification, and need for approval."
-      Rick Rubin

One of my Oud teachers, Ahmad al-Khatib, brilliantly caters each one of his notes with surgical precision. When I asked him about this ability, he told me that his father, a Palestinian poet, used to ask him: "What is eloquence?"

"Eloquence is to convey what you want to the listener in as few and precise words as possible such that they have no doubt about your intentions." Or as Rick Rubin would say, it is about genuine care for all the details.

But also, as the author of _A Creative Act_ states, it is not a vain desire for perfection, but a creative play of what the philosopher Claude Levi-Strauss calls _bricolage_, of working with a limited set of tools to create something completely new.

Alternately, I like Haruki Murakami's quote that "artists are those who can evade the verbose". Together with Einstein, who described creativity as "seeing what everybody else sees and thinking what no one else has thought", sacred perfection in our craft is art within art; the ability to make our audience see the mundane in a new light as we also try to make it work in a larger narrative.

How do you balance between perfection and simplicity in your work? Do you think attention to detail is translatable across genres of art? If so, how might 'evading the verbose' manifest in music or painting?

**Muslim narrates that the Prophet ﷺ said: "Indeed, God
is beautiful and He loves beauty."**

———

"I hold that the perfection of form and beauty is contained in
the sum of all men."
- Albrecht Dürer

We have seen so far that beauty in sound is a necessary catalyst
to unlock the meanings in scripture. Likewise, the translation
of *ihsan* that I personally opt for is 'perfective beauty'.

Just as melody in Qur'an recitation should not be perceived as
mere ornament or decoration, but a medium for
comprehension, similarly beauty in the visual, written and all
forms of art is not mere embellishment, but a vehicle for
understanding.

Much of modern Muslim epistemology – the philosophical
discipline pertaining to knowledge, its sources and methods –
stems from modernist rationalist assumptions that betray the
organic vision of God and universe in Islam.

In no area is this deviation more apparent than the assumption
that art, creativity and beauty are frivolous, simply because they
do not – seem – to serve a utilitarian function. It is all the more

ironic given that the Qur'an uses metaphors, allegories and embellishments of language abundantly.

It is God Himself who commands us to tell stories, so that people might reflect and understand truths and realities that would be incomprehensible if conveyed in any other way.

How do you use beauty as a catalyst for meaning in your work? What truths can be conveyed solely through meetings of colors, words or sounds?

Abu Dawud narrates that the Prophet ﷺ told A'isha: "Indeed, gentleness is never found in something save that it beautifies it, nor is it deprived from something save that it makes it ugly."

———

"The art of gentleness toward ourselves leads to being gentle with others and is a natural prerequisite for our presence with God in prayer."
-      Brennan Manning

Here, the Prophet ﷺ extends the subtlety we explained in the previous hadith, regarding the beauty in art as a catalyst for meaning by including positive traits as sources of beauty.

We may describe the teaching on beauty in this conversation with the Prophet ﷺ as a means of reading people beyond the surface, much as we would appreciate poetry by deciphering its imagery and metaphors.

Any novel or poem contains many layers of meanings, and so do human beings, animals, plants and the entire universe for that matter, as instances of God's Words.

This is what Brennan Manning alludes to by tethering gentleness with oneself and others as a prerequisite for presence with God in prayer: one cannot claim love for the

Author of the universe if they have not shown reverence to His Words. This is emphatically exclaimed in the hadith: "Whoever does not thank people will not thank God" (Ahmad).

56

What is the grammar and eloquence in your craft? What are the metaphors, allegories, imagery, prose and poetry of your medium?

Muslim narrates that the Prophet ﷺ built a pulpit for Hassan b. Thabit in his mosque to recite poetry and defend God and His Messenger ﷺ.

"My role in society, or any artist's or poet's role, is to try and express what we all feel. Not to tell people how to feel. Not as a preacher, not as a leader, but as a reflection of us all."
-    John Lennon

In this hadith, the Prophet ﷺ further affirms the sacrality of art and the role of the artist as a custodian of their faith, no less important than the political leader or religious scholar.

The pulpit in the mosque of the Prophet ﷺ was the liminal space that connected heaven and earth, where revelation transitioned from being an intimate conversation between God and the Prophet ﷺ to entering the public sphere and becoming social policy.

And it is there, in that position, that the Prophet ﷺ chose to grant a voice not to judges, politicians, wealthy people, knowledgeable companions, but Hassan b. Thabit so that he could, as John Lennon states, express how people feel … as a reflection of the entire Muslim community.

This is one prophetic *sunna* (custom) that Muslims today have clearly forsaken. For not only is art education generally outcast from our seminaries and lectures at mosques, but artists are never consulted for their creative intelligence, much less allowed to be custodians of the faith as the Prophet ﷺ intended.

How do you establish a pulpit for your craft in your daily life? Do you perceive yourself as a custodian of your faith? Have you ever contemplated taking ownership of Islam as an artist, what does that entail?

A'isha narrates that the Prophet ﷺ said: "Poetry is speech. The beautiful in it is beautiful and its ugliness is ugly."

———

"The writer, the poet, the novelist, are all creators. This does not mean that they invent language; it means that they use language to create beauty, ideas, images. This is why we cannot do without them."
-   J. M. G. Clezio

In many ways, this hadith is the only proof needed to establish, beyond a doubt, the permissibility of poetry specifically and art generally in Islam.

What is evidently clear is that the Prophet ﷺ sets the criterion for approaching good and bad poetry, whereby not all works in this genre can be dismissed as forbidden.

But what is indirectly established here as well is that just as art cannot be entirely dismissed as forbidden, neither can human speech – even religious discourses and sermons – be accepted wholesale as sacred or beneficial.

It is from this vantage point that the Muslim community should, as Umar advised, 'take itself into account before it is taken into account'. For it is their very abuse of religious edicts that dismiss the talents and creative passions of countless Muslims, leading to a plethora of spiritual and mental ailments – even suicide – that precisely fall under the category of 'ugly speech' in this hadith.

This is especially the case when the community tries to hinder the manifestation of beauty through Muslims who wish to pursue the arts, in favor of more lucrative professions.

Do you take your own art into account often? Do you contemplate the messages behind a particular work? What do you use as a criterion: your own judgment or somebody else's work?

Abu Dawud narrates that Anas said when it rained the Prophet ﷺ went outside and exposed his head and clothing to the rainfall. I asked him: "Why did you do this?" He said: "Because it is *hadith* [a recent arrival] from its Lord."

———

"Let the rain kiss you, let the rain beat upon your head with silver liquid drops. Let the rain sing you a lullaby."
- Langston Hughes

This hadith can be thought of as the heart of this entire book, since the Prophet ﷺ provides the hidden meaning in the very word *hadith* that we alluded to in the introduction.

Whereas this conversation with the Prophet ﷺ highlights the secondary meaning of *hadith*, 'new' or 'recent', Langston Hughes revisits the original meaning of 'conversation', but specifically in the context of a song or lullaby.

This serendipitous meeting behooves us to wander and wonder what kind of *hadith* (conversation) and *dhikr muhdath* (recently arriving remembrance) does rain actually embody. Might it be music as Hughes insinuates?

The Prophet ﷺ is also teaching us to approach and appreciate physical rain, and by extension all divine arrivals, with child-like visceral playfulness, not with our minds through prayers but with our very bodies. To allow it to touch and converse with our scalp and soma as we listen in silence.

What are the proverbial rainfalls in your art and craft? How do you sense and feel these recent conversations? What knowledge do they bring? How does this knowledge sound, look, feel or taste like?

Al-Tirmidhi narrates that the Prophet ﷺ said: "God loves to see the traces of His Bounty on His Servant."

———

"When I work, and in my art, I hold hands with God."
-    Robert Mapplethorpe

Returning to the verse that we discussed in the first chapter: "As for the bounty of your Lord, then proclaim", the Prophet ﷺ in this hadith further establishes the importance of manifesting the bounties and talents that God has given us.

And then, Robert Mapplethorpe shows us the true mark of sincerity and *shukr* (gratitude) needed in proclaiming these Divine Bounties: to hold hands with God.

Such a beautiful image of intimacy highlights that proclaiming God's bounties is less so an attempt to take ownership of the gift and more so acknowledging oneself as a channel for the Divine Breath to move through us uninterrupted.

And herein lies the subtlety of the *shukr* (gratitude) due on art and the artist: we are not grateful for a particular work or even a creative ability but for being chosen as a channel for the Divine Breath.

It is not that our creative ability or art does not matter, but it is to emphasize, as Elizabeth Gilbert mentioned previously, that the muse is external – not internal – to us. The return on this emphatic acknowledgment of our nothingness in the creative process is "If you are grateful, I shall increase you" (14:7).

How do you hold hands with God in your craft? Other than sharing your work publicly, how do you proclaim the bounties of God upon you in your art?

Ahmad narrates that Abu Sa'id al-Khudri said: "The Prophet ﷺ is more bashful than a virgin on her wedding night."

"We are all hungry and thirsty for concrete images. Abstract art will have been good for one thing: to restore its exact virginity to figurative art."
\-   Salvadore Dali

This hadith is one among many that beautifully and importantly problematizes modernist misconstrued notions of masculinity in the Muslim community.

The companion Abu Sa'id al-Khudri did not shy away from painting a feminine image of the Prophet's ﷺ bashfulness. Alongside many other narrations, where his hands ﷺ are described as softer than silk, this authentic portrayal of the Prophet ﷺ reveals a soft dimension needed in true masculinity.

But what is the relationship between this conversation and art or the creative process? The modernist Muslim misperception of masculinity is directly correlated to the view of art as frivolous.

One merely needs to pay attention to the rise of influencers, practically worshipped by Muslim men, who tether a notion of masculinity that degrades women with success in material wealth.

This is but a natural consequence of decades-long reinforcement by the previous generation of Muslim immigrants of economic affluence as a sign of God's Love and Grace. This is how the protestant ethic has fully infiltrated the Muslim psyche.

How would you describe virginity and bashfulness in your work?

Ahmad narrates that the Prophet ﷺ said: "God says: 'I am at My Servant's opinion of Me. So, let them think of Me well.'"

———

"How you draw is a reflection of how you feel about the world. You are not capturing it; you are interpreting it."
-     Juliette Aristides

This is one of the most crucial conversations with the Prophet ﷺ for the artist. My english rendering here intentionally differs from, what I hold to be, a mistranslation of the original Arabic.

Whereas the hadith is usually expressed as: "I'm as My Servant thinks of Me", Ibn al-'Arabi brings our attention to the importance of the preposition *'ind* (at) found in the original Arabic: God is not equivalent to our opinion of Him, but He meets us there.

He limits Himself in the image that we create for Him, and that becomes what Ibn al-'Arabi calls our *wajh khass* (private countenance) and means of communicating with Him.

It is at once an intensely humbling yet liberating feeling to know that we will never know God as He truly is but best as we are. In the former sense, we are rescinded through our inability to envelop Him, while in the latter sense we are reminded of the sacredness of our imagination.

Despite our fragility, He meets us halfway at the shore of our imagination, between the salty water of our finitude and fresh water of His Infinitude. That is where our art is born.

How does your opinion of God manifest in your work? How does He meet you halfway, at the meeting of the two seas, in your words, colors or sounds?

It is narrated that God says: "Whoever loves Me, I love them. Whomever I love, I kill. Whomever I kill, I am their ransom."

—————

"Every book I have written has killed me a little bit more."
-    Norman Mailer

Many Muslim saints like Ibn al-'Arabi delineate between *'ilm* (knowledge) and *hubb* (love) as pertains to the self: whereas the former establishes the ego, the latter seeks to obliterate it.

This is why, in the Qur'an, God humbles the seekers of knowledge by emphasizing that: "Above everyone with knowledge is a knower" (12:76). In other words, those for whom knowledge has become part of their identity (knowers) are a higher rank than those for whom it is simply an attribute.

And yet, we do not find a similar verse reprimanding lovers or stating that "above everyone with love is a lover", simply because love obliterates the ego. This is evident in the very Arabic terms used to describe the actors in the play of love: *habib* means both lover and beloved. Thus, inevitably each will cease to exist in the other.

This is all to say that the journey of the artist, despite its technical dimensions, is ultimately one of love. Picasso alludes to this foregoing of knowledge for the sake of love: "Learn the rules like an amateur, then break them like a professional."

We have already seen what this death of the artist looks like in Jack Lemmon and the art of being and doing nothing to receive and channel everything, whence God Himself is our ransom.

How does annihilation and death of the ego manifest in your art? In turn, how does the return of life emerge afterwards?

Bukhari narrates that the Prophet ﷺ said that God says: "My Servant continues to draw nearer to Me through voluntary acts of worship until I love them. When I love them, I become the sight with which they see, hearing with which they hear, hand with which they strike and foot with which they march."

———

"Art, as far as it is able, follows nature, as a pupil imitates his master. Thus, your art must be, as it were, God's grandchild."
-    Dante Alighieri

This hadith further explores the annihilation of the artist through the path of love. I pray that readers should know by now that I am intentionally liberating these conversations with the Prophet ﷺ from the normal theological and legalistic container within which they have been imprisoned in the West.

I say this because undoubtedly some might complain that this hadith does not speak about artists but rather worshippers. To these readers, I humbly request that you read my previous work *A Nostalgic Remembrance* in order to better understand my approach.

To put it simply: art is the private worship of the artist. And every human being has an inclination and disposition towards a particular craft that God Himself has ingrained in them.

Cultivating that gift is the essence of love and gratitude due to the Giver. When He sees our appreciation of His Gifts, He will bring us closer to mastery which is naught but Him creating through us.

To reiterate: Muslim artists are not obliged to acquiesce to their community's institutions or leaders in forsaking their talents, especially since that contravenes our duty towards God. To Him, and only Him, we owe the responsibility to tread the path towards the summit of mastery.

Have you ever felt God working through you? Do you ever sense that He has heightened your senses to better perceive the contours of your craft?

Al-Tirmidhi narrates that the Prophet ﷺ said that God says: "My Servant, empty yourself for My worship and I will fill you with sufficiency in your chest."

———

"An empty canvas is full."
-    Robert Rauschenberg

It is worth noting that God does not say "sufficiency in wealth", but rather in *sadrak* (your chest). This particular term, *sadr*, is important for Ibn al-'Arabi in his teachings.

As is expected from a creative etymologist like him, he connects this term to the verb *sadara* (to usher forth), in which case the plural of *sadr*, *sudur* (chests), is actually a homonym that has another meaning: ushering forth.

And so, Ibn al-'Arabi connects these two meanings to say that the chest of the human being, where the heart is located, is the place where thoughts and creative imagination ushers forth.

This beautifully contextualizes this hadith qudsi, where God promises to refill an artist's creative well if they focus on worshipping Him. However, as we mentioned, the private worship of the artist is naught but their craft.

For artists, the highest struggle is to trust that our inner well of creativity will never be empty. Do not be afraid of creative dearth or death after the current project or work is complete. He who gifted you the inspiration for this one will do so for the next work as well.

How do you try to entrust your craft and creative inspiration to God? What are some key areas you feel that could benefit from more trust in His Sustenance and Grace?

Ahmad narrates that the Prophet ﷺ said: "If your Lord laughs for the sake of a servant, they will not be judged."

———

"Art must make you laugh a little and make you a little afraid. Anything as long as it doesn't bore."
-    Jean Dubuffet

In another hadith, where the Prophet ﷺ also mentions that God laughs, the companion who narrates the hadith wonders: "And does our Lord laugh?" to which the Prophet ﷺ responded affirmatively. To this the companion replied: "We will never suffer with a Lord who laughs" (Ahmad).

These two, and many other hadiths that mention God laughing are an antidote to an overly – and overtly – dry religiosity that has plagued contemporary Muslim communities in the West. When even *dhikr* (remembrance) is forbidden in groups or in a loud voice, one is left with a stoic faith that is a mere shell of a rich tradition.

But for the artist, as Jean Dubuffet states, laughter is important. And the Muslim artist specifically takes this laughter they experience in their work and that of other artists to try and create a subversion – read sub-version – in a community that has forgotten its heritage.

As Muslim artists, our responsibility towards our community is to never compromise our eccentricity that might very well border on insanity, for that is what makes God laugh.

We are here to remind other Muslims that God does indeed have a sense of humor. Incidentally, there is not a single narration where God is described as crying. Rather, He is either amazed by human actions or laughs for our sake. How do you hope to make God laugh in your work?

Muslim narrates that the Prophet ﷺ said: "God will manifest to people on the Day of Judgment in a form that they do not recognize and will say to them: 'I am your Lord!' to which they will respond: 'We seek refuge in God from you.' Then, He will manifest to them in the form of their creed that they recognize and He will say: 'I am your Lord', which they will affirm."

———

"Art is a reflection of God's Creativity, evidence that we are made in the image of God."
-    Francis Schaeffer

As we will see in the next chapter, this particular hadith is important for Ibn al-'Arabi, and about which he offers an important commentary.

Like many other readers, none of us have probably ever heard this hadith mentioned on the pulpit during Friday sermons or lectures, even though it is an authentic hadith found in Sahih Muslim.

The poignant truth in this conversation is that it is none other than God who is manifesting in the forms of all the creeds of different religions. So what? What is the importance of this for the artist specifically?

If the artist is good at anything, it is 'reeding' meaning at the margins of text, beyond language. Whereas most devout Muslims would focus on the invalidity of those creeds, the artist is deciphering the hidden layer: He is behind all these forms.

And it is precisely the work of the artist to discover – read discover – His presence behind the forms in word, color, or sound. Do you ever find yourself moved to attest to His Presence through immense subtlety and indirection in your work?

Ibn Abi Dunya narrates that the Prophet ﷺ said: "God never grants a servant gratitude and deprives them of increase."

————

"All art arises out of gratitude, a deep pervasive feeling that you are glad something exists outside yourself, that something can complete you."
- 	Dorothy Koppelman

In this conversation, the Prophet ﷺ reveals a secret of *shukr* (gratitude): it itself is a gift from God that needs *shukr*. This cascading contemplation of grace in one's life leads, as Dorothy Koppelman mentions, to a 'deep pervasive feeling you are glad something completes you'.

The artist especially is in the business of gratitude, for lack of a better expression. This is because they create with their bodies that which is itself an expression of gratitude, since creativity is the closest imitation of God and, thus, the highest form of flattery.

And this also returns us to our discussion on gratitude above and the responsibility of trusting that the flow of Divine Inspiration will continue beyond any given work or project.

It is important to understand that so many voices around us, despite being well-intentioned, try to convince us otherwise. Family, community and society all attempt to instill fear in us of the abysses in our creative journey.

We listen respectfully, ignore dutifully and continue to jump into the unknown … because nobody else will do it for everybody's sake except us. How do you show gratitude in your work for the craft and the raft of gratitude itself?

Ahmad narrates that the Prophet ﷺ said: "If you were always as you are with me then angels would shake your hands as you walk in the alleyways. But [your states] should fluctuate every other hour."

"Art is never finished, only abandoned."
-   Leonardo Da Vinci

The artist's journey is one of mastering the art of letting go at every level of craft and life. This includes the need to accept that just as a creative block is not permanent, so is the case for creative flow.

We work as diligently when the holy spirit is there to support us as when it is nowhere to be found. In truth, however, it is still there, just hiding and not making itself known. But why would it not make its presence felt?

Because as in the universal worship, *salat*, where we must consciously eliminate *riya'*, or the ostentatious desire for other than God, so must we also gift our entire craft and artwork to God.

But this is not a superficial display of piety, but rather a confrontation with oneself as we stand over the abyss of emptiness in the well of creativity. Are we working diligently only because the inspiration is there? Does He not deserve our gratitude for the gift of art? And for realizing the very need to work?

As Da Vinci beautifully states, art is never finished only abandoned. What is His Presence in your craft save the calling itself? How do you remain diligent in your productivity despite the ebb and flow of creative inspiration?

Bukhari and Muslim narrate that the Prophet ﷺ said: "Indeed, actions are by intentions."

———

"All art is intentional, not incidental, and therefore art does not happen by accident, even if artists are willing to exploit accidents."
- Ryan and Jacob Muldowney

The Prophet ﷺ also said in another hadith that "the intention of the believer is better than their action" (Tabarani). But what does that intention actually look or sound like? Is it a single prayer recited silently at a specific moment in time or an incessant movement?

This is particularly important for the artist, as brothers Ryan and Jacob Muldowney explain. And I feel that for the poet, painter, musician, filmmaker and chef intention is best described as presence, of the same type that Richard Misrach had with his surroundings.

The artist's intention is a never-ending *sama'* (audition) and deep listening for a *masjid* (site of prostration) in the world. This requires the trust of which we previously spoke. Just as we have conviction that the Giver will continue His Gifts inwardly, so will they also remain outwardly, as markers that speak to the traces within us.

It is worth noting that the Arabic word *niyya*, intention, is phonetically related to *nayy* (raw) (e.g., meat). This eloquently describes how our creative presence in the world needs to be particularly tethered to the unexpected, for that is where God will most likely reveal Himself.

How would you express your intention as an artist? Try to describe this in terms that are not religious but either using the technical vocabulary of your craft or a more universal vision.

Bukhari narrates that the Abu al-Darda' said to the Prophet ﷺ that Salman al-Farisi said to him: "Your Lord has a right upon you, your family has a right upon you as does your soul. So, give everyone who has a right upon you their right." The Prophet ﷺ said: "Salman was truthful."

———

"The threefold responsibility of the artist is: to creation, the
individual talent, and to humanity."
-    Charles Philip Brooks

The quote by Charles Philip Brooks here beautifully contextualizes the responsibilities of that artist, especially in the present day and age.

Then, for the Muslim artist, we must be emphatic that in traditional Muslim societies, when art was seen as a necessity for the spiritual health of both individual and the collective, it was never the responsibility of artists themselves to make a 'living' from their work.

Rather, the artist's sole focus is to 'live' their craft and the community's prerogative to make sure they are financially capable of doing that, not only for their own sake as artists but for the community's at large. This is because, as we mentioned, artists are the storytellers of their people.

I have previously mentioned during lectures and conversations that not every artist should be practicing their craft full-time, but if all artists in a community are part-time artists, that demographic is in a deep creative and spiritual crisis.

How do you set the boundaries of the responsibilities towards God through your craft and art? How do you make your responsibilities known to others around you who still think that your passion is a frivolous hobby?

Al-Tirmidhi narrates that the Prophet ﷺ said: "Ask your Lord for all your needs, even salt for your food and the sole of your sandals if it is ruined."

———

"I inhaled the fragrance of cedar as fresh as the first day that I acquired the guitar. And a voice seemed to say to me, "You are an old man and you have not said thank you; you have not brought your gratitude back to the soil from which this fragrance arose." And so, I come here tonight to thank the soil and the soul of this people that has given me so much."
-     Leonard Cohen

Like Brooks' statement in the previous conversation, Leonard Cohen also provides an eloquent interpretation to the prophetic wisdom here: the artist need not only seek God's aid in every word, brush stroke, cadence of sound, frame of reel or salt in their art, but also to recognize the myriad of causes and means through which Divine Care has reached them.

If we have been emphasizing the need to focus on God as a show of gratitude in our craft, the inward reality of this responsibility is that the entire world around us, which is our canvas and palette as artists, is naught but His Manifestations.

We seek Him for the salt in our craft and then open ourselves to the countless and unexpected ways in which He will deliver that to us, at the hands of a saint, paint or a heart broken of taint. And as we receive all these as His Manifestations, we perceive them once again back towards their original source.

That is our *tawhid* as artists: just all words return to ink, colors to dye, music to sound so must the entire world that speaks of ideas and projects also turn back to the peak of Divinity.

How does *tawhid* emanate in your work and craft? Do you ever consciously, whether outwardly or inwardly, try to root the myriad of people and things in the world back to God?

God says: "I was a Hidden Treasure and loved to be known. Thus, I created creation that I may be known by them."

———

"And you have treasures hidden within you—extraordinary treasures—and so do I, and so does everyone around us. And bringing those treasures to light takes work and faith and focus and courage and hours of devotion, and the clock is ticking, and the world is spinning, and we simply do not have time anymore to think so small."
-    Elizabeth Gilbert

This is perhaps the most widely transmitted prophetic conversation among Muslim saints, including Ibn al-'Arabi; one that is specifically verified via *kashf* (unveiling), not *naql* (transmitted sources) or *'aql* (rational reflection).

I have also dedicated an entire chapter titled "On the Hidden Treasure" to this conversation in *A Nostalgic Remembrance*. What we have outlined there are five stages of the creative process, from creative block to externalization of the creative inspiration in a living and breathing work of art.

As Elizabeth Gilbert – who serendipitously uses the exact term found in the hadith 'hidden treasure' – states, every human being has this veiled trove. However, it is the artist who reminds humanity of their own inner gifts by undertaking the arduous journey to awaken and excavate theirs.

Here, we emphasize a crucial point: the arts are not only a collection of crafts and products, but also a metaphor, process and blueprint for being, otherwise called the 'art of living'. The artist, in their trek towards the summit, reminds the rest of us how to be human.

How do you find your hidden treasure? What strategies have you developed to wade and wait through the difficult periods of creative block?

The Prophet ﷺ is narrated to have said: "Whoever knows their own self, has already known their Lord."

————

"I don't paint dreams or nightmares; I paint my own reality."
-    Frida Kahlo

This particular narration of this conversation is offered by Ibn al-'Arabi, in contrast to the usually transmitted version: "Whoever knows their own self, will know their Lord."

The change in emphasis by Ibn al-'Arabi makes a drastic difference in meaning, equating knowledge of self with that of God, as He is and will always be for us as individuals.

This is a return to the previous conversation in this chapter, "I am at My Servant's opinion of Me. So let them think of Me well." No craft is better and more efficient at attaining knowledge of self and, in turn, God than art.

If an artwork is the body, then the creative process is its spirit. Both these aspects of the artist's journey reveal to them who they are, will be and the contours of God's presence in their lives within every inkblot, aroma of dye and aging sound in their compositions.

Thus, Frida Kahlo says that every painting she's made have been nothing but her own reality. But she also alludes to a subtlety, that once we perceive the art we make as our inner reality, it ceases to be a dream or nightmare; it simply is.

This Mevlana Rumi described in a previous conversation as "a field beyond belief and unbelief" where he "will meet" us. How does knowledge of God and self emerge in your work? How does your art help you transcend the distinction between difficulty and ease, evil and good, light and darkness in life?

God is narrated to have said: "Neither My Heavens nor Earth can encompass Me, save only the heart of My Believing Servant."

———

"All great artists draw from the same source: the human heart, which tells us that we are all more alike than we are unalike."
-    Maya Angelou

The word *heart* contains so much. One can find *art*, *hear* and *ear* immediately embraced withing this word. However, with some digging we also come across some smaller anagrams, such as *tear*, *earth* and *hearth*.

As Ibn al-'Arabi reminds us constantly, connections in language are never coincidental, but always a co-incidence and alignment between word and world. In this case, he also focuses on the word for 'heart' in Arabic, *qalb* and its connections.

Whereas the *'aql*, which might be roughly translated as 'rational faculty', pays homage to *'iqal* (leash) and limitation, the *qalb* is not only a noun but also a *masdar* (verbal noun or gerund) meaning upending or fluctuation.

This Ibn al-ʿArabi uses to highlight that the heart is the only human faculty capable of surfing the ocean of Divine Manifestations, whereas the *ʿaql* is bound to categories and definitions that betray the reality of existence.

It should not be surprising then that Maya Angelou regards the heart as the resource for all art. For the creative process is nothing but capturing a single moment as we sail across these waves of Theophanies. What aspects of your heart do you feel are most present in your work? Your feelings, emotions, heartbeats or something else?

Ibn Majah narrates that when the Prophet ﷺ migrated to Madinah, little girls from the tribe of Bani Najjar came to him and sang: "We are little girls from Bani Najjar, how wonderful is Muhammad as a *jār* (neighbor)." He smiled and said to them: "God knows I love you."

———

"Before a child speaks, it sings. Before they write, they paint. As soon as they stand, they dance. Art is the basis of human expression."
- Phylicia Rashad

In another narration of this conversation, the Prophet ﷺ asks these young girls after they sing for him ﷺ: "Do you love me?" to which they respond affirmatively. Then, he ﷺ gives the response above: "God knows I love you."

And this would not be the first instance in which he ﷺ asks someone this beautiful question: "Do you love me?" He ﷺ directed it also at his confidante Abu Bakr during their migration from Mecca to Madinah when the latter was worried for his friend's safety in the desert.

Without a doubt, he ﷺ already knew that Abu Bakr and these young girls from Madinah love him immensely. However, by asking them this question he ﷺ wanted them to exorcise their emotions because he ﷺ knew the importance of alleviating the pressure of love and the intense feelings they exercise upon the heart.

Perhaps, just as he ﷺ sought to expose his head and body to rainfall, a recent arrival from God, he likewise hoped to expose his heart to children who are also a proverbial rainfall, recently arriving from God's Presence.

Perhaps it is for this reason that, as Phylicia Rashad mentions, children sing and dance before writing and reading, since that is the language and movement of heavens. How do you try to return to a child-self during your creative process?

Al-Tirmidhi narrates that the Prophet ﷺ said: "By God, if you were to lower a man with a rope to the lowest earth, they would descend upon God."

"When I judge art, I take my painting and put it next to a God made object like a tree or flower. If it clashes, it is not art."
-   Paul Cezanne

Ibn al-'Arabi often quotes an earlier Muslim saint Abu Sa'id al-Kharraz who when asked: "Where did you find God?" he responded by saying: "At the meeting of opposites." That is the point where the *'aql* slumbers and *qalb* awakens.

This is also the point that T.S. Eliot alluded to in *Dry Salvages*: "But the intersection of the timeless with time, that is an occupation for a saint." It is Alice's Wonderland, almost verbatim as Ibn al-'Arabi describes a vision where he sailed across a sea of sand in a ship made from stone.

Unsurprisingly, this meeting of opposites is the land of imagination, dreams, mystical visions and creativity. And it is there that as the Prophet ﷺ states, you can lower a rope and it would descend upon God, who is otherwise entirely unbound by time and space. Rather, He is the Creator of time and space.

How do we understand this perplexity, paradox and seeming contradiction? We do not. Instead, we stand under it and listen. However, Ibn al-'Arabi gives us an allusion that God must necessarily appear in limited forms since to insinuate that He cannot manifest within the images of time and space is itself a limitation upon His Absolution.

How do you find the presence of God inside the very boundaries of your colors, sounds and words? Have you ever felt your canvas, poem or composition descend – not ascend – into the Divine Presence?

Muslim narrates that Anas b. Malik said: "I neither smell musk nor perfume sweeter than the fragrance of the Prophet ﷺ. Nor did I touch silk softer than him ﷺ." Another companion asked Anas: "You can almost see the Messenger ﷺ now and hear his melody, can you not?" Anas said: "Yes, by God, I can!"

———

"Love is a perfume you cannot pour onto others without getting a few drops on yourself."
-       Ralph Waldo Emerson

Like other conversations in this section, which one would never hear from pulpits today despite being of the most authentic *isnad* (chain of transmission), the second part of this conversation is never mentioned by scholars or preachers.

And yet, it is perhaps the most consequential component of the hadith that carries its entire spirit. This is not to say that the first part, where Anas b. Malik praises the Prophet's ﷺ aroma and softness, is not important. However, one can find such expressions of love abundantly in many narrations.

What is of creative significance in the second part is that both Anas and his interlocutor reveal to us the relationship between memory and the senses. By *tadhakkur* (remembering) – itself the essence of *dhikr* (remembrance) – the fragrance and physical touch of the Prophet ﷺ, Anas was able to reignite his *dhikra* (memory) ﷺ into a *hadra* (presence) that can be seen and felt.

More than that, there is a remarkable association between fragrance and melody. Incidentally, the contemporary Indian saint and musician Inayat Khan believed fragrance and melody to be adjacent penultimate realms preceding the Divine Presence.

Which of your five senses are most active in your craft? Which of them do you feel are the mediums through which you communicate your memories and, in turn, write your memoirs?

Ahmad narrates that the Prophet ﷺ said: "This religion began as a stranger and will return a stranger. So, glad tidings be to the strangers." It was asked: "Who are the strangers?" He ﷺ said: "Those exiled from their tribes."

———

"Art is the closest we can come to understanding how a stranger really feels."
- Roger Ebert

What a suitable conversation with which to conclude this section. Like the previous one, the second part of this hadith is also omitted often from contemporary Muslim teachings.

This is not surprising, since there is a subconscious awareness among the paragons of mainstream religious discourse in the Muslim community that they are in fact the ones who have exiled the strangers in our day and age.

And no other group has been more exiled and marginalized from the mosque, seminary, Islamic education and as formative custodians of their faith and community than Muslim artists. And yet, as members of the art world, they are the last reminder and remainder from an ancient world.

The artist reminds us how humanity used to create meaning, through creativity and imagination, prior to the advent of the industrial revolution, enlightenment and worship of slogans like the 'age of reason' and 'knowledge triumphant'.

In other words, and as Roger Ebert concurs, artists are in many ways the strangers who are exiled from their tribes and who remind us how faith began and how it has returned today to that primordial original state, rare yet organic.

How often do you feel like a stranger in your community and family? How would you describe your art as a safe space on the margins?

Chapter Two: *Ibn al-'Arabi*

"Reality is perplexity. Perplexity is anxiety and movement, and movement is life."

———

"A successful work of art is not one which resolves contradictions in a spurious harmony, but one which expresses the idea of harmony negatively by embodying the contradictions, pure and uncompromised, in its innermost structure."
- Theodore Adorno

Nothing is living save that it is moving, as Ibn al-'Arabi explains. Hence, to perform ablution, one must wash using running – not still – water. The reason is not simply that still water carries filth, but rather that it is spiritually dead.

And so, so long as we are moving, both inwardly and outwardly, we are alive. But what exactly causes us to move? As Ibn al-'Arabi explains, it is perplexity, contention and creative tension.

In many ways, this is yet another antidote for a stoic Islamic religiosity today that tries, as Theodore Adorno explains, to 'resolve contradictions in a spurious harmony'. The wholesale adoption – not even adaptation – of rational positivism has rendered faith a corporate affair.

Religious education is reduced to its rational dimensions and that which can be institutionalized and graded. Meanwhile, negotiating the messiness of life with the sacred, usually the prerogative of art, is no where to be found.

How do you embrace contradiction in your work? How do you balance between offering closure and maintaining the tension for a possible continuity and climax in the narratives you weave within your craft?

"From the darknesses of ignorance to the light of guidance and darkness of perplexity."

"Film as dream, film as music. No art passes our conscience in the way film does, and goes directly to our feelings, deep down into the dark rooms of our souls."
-    Ingmar Bergman

"The dark side of the force is a pathway to many abilities, some consider to be unnatural", says Darth Sidious to Anakin Skywalker in *Star Wars: Revenge of the Sith*. The allure of the absence of light is the fabric from which every villainy is weaved.

And yet, as Ibn al-'Arabi shows, not every darkness is the same. Here he relies on a hadith qudsi where God is described as having 70,000 veils of light and darkness. If He were to lift them, then the Light of His Countenance would burn all that is in existence.

This appreciation of darkness, especially in art, is much needed in today's discourse on creativity in the Muslim community. The blanket condemnation of artworks that contain any trace of evil or darkness reveals a complete lack of awareness of storytelling, even as it unfolds in the Qur'an.

Darkness must be allowed to unfurl in the world of a play so that it does not overflow into the play of the world. This is precisely why art exists: to allow us to spill blood in ink, color and sound as a sacrifice that suffices our bodies from misery.

In the Qur'an, God allows satan and pharaoh to speak and state their claims. And yet, despite His command to 'tell stories', the Muslim community continues to marginalize into oblivion narratives of the brokenhearted.

What role does darkness play in your work? How do you entertain it and allow unseemly characters to make their claims? Do you feel that this is therapeutic for you as an artist?

"Every human being with an imagination, when they imagine, their gaze extends to the Divine Imagination."

———

"The world of reality has its limits; the world of imagination is boundless."
-    Jean-Jacques Rousseau

This statement by Ibn al-'Arabi is one of the reasons why I hold him to be a necessary companion, not only for Muslim but also non-Muslim artists. His expansive and universal embrace of all human imagination is a necessary lens for our day and age. Note that the Andalusian mystic does not limit this ability, to tap into the Divine Imagination, to Muslims or even those who believe in God. Rather, it is open to all humanity. This delivers us to the debate of high vs. low art and the different sources of creative inspiration.

As I have explained elsewhere, Ibn al-'Arabi emphasizes here that the source of every creative inspiration can only be Divine Imagination. However, this does not preclude the possibility of low art, with a few caveats. First, low art is simply a pure creative inspiration that was mistranslated into an external work of art, due to many possible reasons such as trauma or social conditioning. However, whereas deeming a work as entirely satanic requires its destruction, one that is seen as a mistranslation simply needs healing. Secondly, to decide that an artwork is low or high one must first have a deep appreciation for the society and culture in which it is produced.

Many Muslims in the West, even some who produce 'sacred art' like Islamic calligraphy, regard indigenous art forms such as jazz, hip hop or the blues as satanic. In reality, these genres are not only sacred, but are the very memory of the Sacred in the West.

How do you engage with indigenous memories in your work? What responsibility do you feel you have in your art to acknowledge the embrace of all humanity in Divine Imagination?

"Images and statues have been forbidden in Islam because God wants us to activate our imagination, as has come in the authentic narration: 'Worship God as though you see Him'."

―――――

"In art, the hand can never execute anything higher than the heart can imagine."
- Ralph Waldo Emerson

We return to imagination, which we discussed in previous chapters. Ibn al-'Arabi describes *khayal* (imagination) as a realm where 'bodies are spiritualized and spirits are embodied'. This is the meeting point between the fresh and salty waters of spirit and body at the *barzakh* (liminal interstice).

This means that imagination is also the land of *hayra* (perplexity) where opposites meet and a rope may descend upon God. This is Alice's Wonderland where the artist ventures to find inspiration for their next project.

And, for some, they never leave this *ard al-haqiqa* (land of reality) ― as Ibn al-'Arabi alternately calls it ― and they are always chasing the white rabbit.

Therefore, the censure against physical images of God and the Prophet ﷺ in Islam is not as some perceive it, a limitation, but rather a liberation. Not to mention that even physical portrayals of the Prophet ﷺ have been celebrated for centuries in art forms like miniature paintings.

Nevertheless, as we have seen in the previous chapter, *ihsan* requires us to imagine God during our worship. It is here that both Ibn al-'Arabi and Ralph Waldo Emerson agree that the physical must give way for the imaginal to roam free.

Do physical forms always blind and bind your imagination? Or do you ever experience instances where the boundaries of the physical are a safe space for you to explore in the land of imagination?

"I have opened for you the *i'tibar* (taking heed). It is the passage from the form which manifests in the physical domain to what is related in your essence, or at the Side of al-*Haqq* [the Real]: that which signifies God. This is the figurative meaning of *i'tibar*. It is like "You have *'abarta* (crossed over) the valley when you traversed it."

He made this life a *'ibrah* [example], or bridge that is *yu'bar* [crossed]. This means that it should be *tu'abbar* [to be interpreted], just as dreams that human beings see, while sleeping, are interpreted."

———

"Art-making has an alchemical effect on the imagination. It awakens the senses and sharpens insights, teaching us to think in symbols, metaphors, and to de-code complexity, so we can perceive the world in new ways."
-    Linda Naiman

This is one of the most remarkable organic visions of Ibn al-'Arabi, where he begins from language and transitions to dreams and art to give us a creative appreciation of the universe.

His eloquence and sophistication is indirectly summarized by Linda Naiman who highlights that the process of 'art-making teaches us to perceive the world in new ways.'

This we have emphasized before, that the arts are not mere crafts or products but more importantly a process of making meaning, perceiving and receiving the world around us at a level deeper than the surface. To linger continuously at the 'field beyond belief and unbelief', as Mevlana Rumi describes, is precisely this creative state and way of being.

Inversely, the obsession with rational positivism and restricting faith to legal edicts and dialectical theology has lead many in the Muslim community to live digital lives, fluctuating between the 1 of *halal* (licit) and 0 of *haram* (illicit).

What are your various acts of *'ubur* (crossing over) in your craft? How is your *'ibarah* (expressions) and *'ibrah* (parables) married in the very technical details of your work?

"The world is so called, *'alam* because it is an *'alamah* [sign] that points to the *'alim* [knower], who is God"

———

"I use symbols to imply abstract ideas. My main objective is to construct a synthesis of the natural, the abstract, and the imaginary, and so bring into existence a language of personal symbolism."
-    Kent Addison

As we said in the previous conversation, the creative process is more than products and beauty that is felt with the senses, but more importantly a process through which we may come to learn about the 'art of living'.

This is a point that Ibn al-'Arabi recurringly visits in his writings: how to think creatively. He himself utilizes a thoroughly innovative etymology, as we have seen, that constructs an entire metaphysics based on the grammatical and phonetic relationships between words.

Here, he reveals one such connection between *'alam* (world), *'alamah* (sign) and *'alim* (God as Knower). In turn, to have *'ilm* (knowledge) of anything in the *'alam* (world) is to decipher its reality as an *'alamah* (sign) that points to the *'alim* (Knower).

Transcending the reality of things as mere material entities towards their spiritual significance is also the frontier of the artist. It is from this perspective, then, that artists are true *'ulama* (knowers) according to Ibn al-'Arabi.

For artists, we try to communicate with the world around us in the language of feelings in a way that does not dismiss the material plane but enhances it. It is here that the Muslim artist specifically has much to contribute to the way Islam as a faith is practiced: not by neglecting the body and physical world but acknowledging and sacralizing its suffering. How do you engage with the world as a matrix of signs in your work? What do these symbols look like once translated onto your canvas?

"Jesus was only able to resurrect the dead, cure the leper and bring a clay bird to life through breath in human form, because that is the image that the holy spirit Gabriel took when he cast the Word of God to Mary, through breath as well."

"I chose faces and figures as my subject matter simply due to the fact that the human form is already beautiful art."
-    Frank Bruno

Continuing with our emphasis on the importance of the physical form, Ibn al-'Arabi makes this clear here in the case of Jesus. He tethers Christ's ability to perform miracles to his – imaginal – physical form, since that is the image that the holy spirit appeared in when he cast the Word to Mary.

He continues to say that had Gabriel appeared in any other form, including his original angelic image, Christ would have to appear in that form in order to perform any miracle. Why does Ibn al-'Arabi place such an emphasis on Jesus' physical form?

Because unlike modern religious sensibilities that try to dismiss the physical form as a hindrance and obstacle from reaching true spiritual nirvana, Ibn al-'Arabi – and countless other

Muslim and non-Muslim saints — want us to understand the importance of the body in our journey.

However, it is not just the body but also all its eccentricities and habits, fragilities and weaknesses. These are all *'alamat* (signs) and windows into our spiritual dispositions.

The artist, whose very palette is the physical word, color or sound, is charged with this incredible responsibility of highlighting the sanctity of form. How do you accomplish this task in your work and craft? What is the sacredness of form in your art?

"Poetry is so called, *shi'r*, because it is related to *sha'ar* [hair] and *shu'ur* [intuition]. Just as you can feel your hand close to your body without actually touching it by the reaction of the hair on your skin."

———

"Poetry is the revelation of a feeling that the poet believes to be interior and personal which the reader recognizes as his own."
-    Salvatore Quasimodo

Ibn al-'Arabi resorts to etymology once again for a metaphysical excursion and to sacralize poetry, tethering it to our focus in the previous conversation: emotions and feelings.

Elsewhere, the Andalusian mystic explains that the Qur'an is not poetry only because scripture contains laws that must be expressed clearly in prose, not using the ambiguous language of poetry.

Ibn al-'Arabi even describes a vision where he was given the reality and support of the muse of poetry, which in turn inspired the quote above. He saw himself swallowing a single hair of light that descended to his stomach then emerged from his mouth as a dragon that filled the horizons.

Taking all of this, the crucial remark in Ibn al-'Arabi's quote is, once again, his emphasis on the body whereby *shi'r* (poetry) is tethered to *sha'ar* (hair) and *shu'ur* (feelings).

The poet's – and artist's – ability to communicate at this level of body and feelings is highlighted beautifully by Salvatore Quasimodo. Art does not address us at the level of mind or rationality but heart, emotions and spirit.

How conscious are you of the feelings and emotions you seek to evoke in your audience through your craft? What are some strategies you utilize for that purpose?

"Regarding the hadith narrated by Muslim that God will reveal Himself in the forms of all creeds on the Day of Judgment, whence people will deny Him in the forms they do not recognize and affirm only the form of their creed, the knowers will stand behind the masses and affirm all the forms, proclaiming with each manifestation: 'You are our Lord!'"

———

"Whereas life separates meaning from emotion, art unites them. Story is an instrument by which you create such epiphanies at will, the phenomenon known as aesthetic emotion...Life on its own, without art to shape it, leaves you in confusion and chaos, but aesthetic emotion harmonizes what you know with what you feel to give you a heightened awareness and a sureness of your place in reality."
-       Robert McKee

Ibn al-'Arabi returns us here to the conversation with the Prophet ﷺ narrated by Muslim wherein God appears according to all the different creeds on the Day of Judgment. Between the Andalusian mystic and Robert McKee, we have here a resounding reformulation of the *tawhid* (monotheism) of the artist.

As Ibn al-'Arabi shows, the mission of the knowers is one of recognizing and proclaiming the *'alamah* (sign) of the *'alim* (Knower) in the *'alam* (world). Meanwhile, McKee gives us a more personal and intimate portrayal of this process, where art 'unites meaning with emotion'.

What art provides us with is an entirely new way of perceiving *tawhid*, not as a mental exercise of 'believing that God is one', but rather an active process of making that oneness take place, by rooting the entire matrix of signs in the signified.

But that is ultimately what the artist does, creating meaning and emotion out of chaos, as McKee explains. In turn, art is the playground where *tawhid* can be truly tasted. How do you experience, capture and convey this resounding oneness in your work?

"Poets have extinguished their words about existent things. This one writes about women, the other about wealth, fame or status. But the knowers see only the One behind all these forms, only Him."

———

"Poetry is the art of uniting pleasure with truth."
-    Samuel Johnson

Bringing the previous conversations about *tawhid* and poetry together, Ibn al-'Arabi encourages us here to undertake the journey of *tawhid* in poetry, specifically to perceive the myriad of topics about which poets write as being none other than God.

Once again, Ibn al-'Arabi's companion in this conversation, Samuel Johnson, gives an apt description of this *tawhid* due for poetry: to unite pleasure with truth. Note that he uses the term pleasure as opposed to joy, which is perceived as a higher form of meaningful happiness.

In other words, Johnson is emphasizing that poetry, and by extension all art, is really about sacralizing what appears as mundane and profane. It should not be difficult to perceive stoic joy as truth, but the challenge is to see love for 'women, wealth and status' as a longing for God.

And so, once again, we have the affirmation that art and artists are paragons of *tawhid* as pertains to our life in this world, its toils, turmoil, sufferings and redemptions.

By creating a meaningful story out of chaos, the artist gives hope where none seems possible in sight. This alleviation of disconnection towards some sense of cohesion amidst the chaos is itself the *tawhid* that renders art a necessity in every age.

How much do you try to connect what is dissonant and disparate in your work? What benefit or joy does that provide you as an artist? Do you make this pronounced or hidden for the viewer to find on their own?

"The letters of language are nations from among those that God created. Calligraphy is their skeleton, diacritics their skin and accents come as the Divine Breath that brings them to life."

———

"Your letters are birds. Caught in your net, stirred from their flight... Their wings are our written down speech. Landing and takeoff is conducted according to the rules. The rules you call grammar, but it is nothing other than geometry."
- 	Jasna Horvat

Ibn al-'Arabi's teachings, I feel, are a doorway to an ancient world. He allows us, with such nuance, to appreciate how people in the past approached language, art, faith and life. While there are many authors before and during his time, Ibn al-'Arabi is unique in his prolific career and his many works that remain available today.

What he explains, and Jasna Horvat beautifully elaborates upon, is how I personally approach my native tongue of Arabic. As an Oud musician, first and foremost, and poet secondly, I am much more interested in the meanings dormant in the shapes and sounds of letters than those assigned by grammar.

The Oud and Arabic music delivered me to this realization, that my love for words relates to their sounds, not their bindings in dictionaries.

To read calligraphy and listen to the sound of words is to return to a time immemorial when language was itself art, not merely a means to express art. The artist reminds us of that moment, when ancient Egyptians drew their meanings using shapes, as Horvat explains.

Do you often think about the contours of meaning in your work? How do you feel notions like grammar and eloquence manifest specifically in your craft?

"A *sama'* [audition] that only moves human emotions is limited, whereas that which results in *ma'rifa* [gnosis] is an absolute Divine Audition."

———

"After silence, that which comes nearest to expressing the inexpressible is music."
-      Aldous Huxley

Ibn al-'Arabi further sanctifies human emotions as a medium for receiving, perceiving and conveying the Sacred. What he says in this conversation is not that feelings are unimportant during musical audition, but that they must be understood as a language.

In other words, we have to be present emotionally, as a necessary prerequisite for reaching the Divine Presence, especially through art. To this end, Aldous Huxley agrees and expresses this truth as music being the 'nearest medium after silence that is able to convey the inexpressible'.

In both the Qur'an and Old Testament, one finds a consecration of silence with God. Verses such as "Voices were silenced for the Most-Merciful, whence you hear only whispers" (20:108) – in the Qur'an – and "Be still and know that I am God" (Psalm 46:10) highlight a subtle communication that occurs at the level of silence.

This is perhaps why 'silent' and 'listen' are anagrams in English, whereas *samt* (silence) and *sawt* (sound) in Arabic differ in only one letter. And it is the very experience of music that allows us to journey inwardly to the presence of silence and listening.

I am always amazed at the fact that I can remain absolutely silent for so long while I play the Oud. Perhaps if a community of faith truly wanted to instill meditative practices in their members, they should encourage them to learn a musical instrument.

How does *sama'* (audition) manifest in your craft? Do you ever find yourself listening in the very process of making art?

**"The four strings of the Oud correspond to the four
human humors: blood, phlegm and two biles."**

———

"We are all instruments endowed with feeling and memory.
Our senses are so many strings that are struck by surrounding
objects and that also frequently strike themselves."
-      Denis Diderot

As we will see in the last chapter of this book, there were

companions of the Prophet ﷺ who played the Oud; a tradition

that continued well until the 17th century when renowned

Muslim polymaths taught music theory in Mecca and Medina

and even held concerts in the vicinities of the two holy

precincts.

To continue with the previous conversation, as Huxley

expressed and Denis Diderot does here as well, music alludes

to meanings that are beyond the prison of rationalism and

logic. Diderot specifically humanizes musical, especially string,

instruments.

And this is precisely what Ibn al-'Arabi does as well by

constructing an analogy between the strings of the Oud and

four human humors, which were the basis of bodily

equilibrium and health in ancient medicine.

Of course, we human beings have our own bodily musical instrument: our vocal system, which happens to be both a wind and string instrument. This by itself renders any argument against the permissibility of music and musical instruments irrelevant.

However, I propose also that we look at musical instruments as sages that teach the musician how to become like them: empty yet full of sound, nothing and thus able to channel the Divine Breath.

How does sound function in your craft? Do you feel any relationship between music or musical instruments and the art you make?

"Saints are two ranks in their *himma*. The lower are those who set their imagination on an intelligible entity in the spiritual realm and can project it into physical existence but have to maintain their gaze upon it for it to subsist. On the other hand, the higher-ranking saints need not maintain their gaze upon it for it to subsist."

———

"The purpose of art is to raise people to a higher level of awareness than they would otherwise attain on their own."
-       Brassai

I would like to borrow a trick from Ibn al-'Arabi and resort to etymology for a moment to excavate subtleties in the notion of *himma* (intentive power).

The most immediate relationship that emerges is that with *hamm* (burden). Incidentally, Ibn al-'Arabi uses a similar term, *karb* (constriction), as he provocatively tries to explain the reason why God created the universe.

The immense creative potential within the Divine Essence led to this *karb ilahi* (Divine Constriction) and need for all the potentialities within to unfold. However, Ibn al-'Arabi emphasizes that this constriction was not an attribute of the Divine Essence but rather the essences of the created things within.

By granting these essences of the created things permission to manifest on the canvas of existence, Ibn al-'Arabi says that God *naffasa* (alleviated) their *karb* (constriction) through *Nafas al-Rahman* (breath of the Most-Merciful), which is the light of the Prophet ﷺ.

Our creative process, as human beings, is a constant re-enactment of this original Divine Movement. We direct our *himma* to art in order to alleviate the *hamm* (creative tension) that resides within us, thereby following God's *sunna* (custom). How do you feel that your creative process may be a form of alleviation, not only of difficulties but also creative potential? How do you try to become aware of the life that you channel into existence through your art?

"Saints are two ranks according to their knowledge of self. The lower gain knowledge of self as they pay attention to rotation of the heavenly orbits and how that affects them. Once they obtain full knowledge of self, and reach the higher rank, they come to know what will happen to them, even the moment of death."

———

"Art is the stored honey of the human soul."
-    Theodore Dreiser

Here, Ibn al-'Arabi reveals another hierarchy of sainthood, based on self-knowledge. If in the previous conversation the two ranks of *himma* delineate a projection of our inner potential upon the world, this soliloquy highlights the opposite direction, whereby we draw a self-portrait from the world around us.

Ibn al-'Arabi is indirectly drawing the attention of the contemporary artist to the fact that our craft does not live and thrive in a vacuum. Ours is an organic existence, no matter how much modernist rationalism and contemporary religious education, which is an extension of this project, try to convince us otherwise.

Ironically, despite the absence in the current religious discourse of this embrace of the sacred in the world, we find it clearly outlined in the Qur'an: "We shall show them Our Signs in the horizons and in their own selves, until it is clear to them that it/he/He is the Truth" (41:53).

And just as *'ilm* (knowledge) is married to the *'alamah* (sign) of the *'alim* (Knower) in the *'alam* (world), so is *ayah* (sign) in the above married to *ayah* (verse). Thus, if this existence is but a uni-verse, is there any doubt as to whether it is Divine Prose or Poetry?

How does self-knowledge manifest for you in your craft? Did you ever transition in your work from knowing yourself after a work is completed to the reverse process, where you knew how a work will conclude because you know your dispositions as an artist?

"God says: 'He merged the two seas they meet. The fresh and salty waters represent the spiritual and physical realms respectively, while the imaginal world is the *barzakh* between them."

———

"In the universe, there are things that are known, and things that are unknown, and in between them, there are doors."
-   William Blake

Returning us to this verse that we discussed previously, Ibn al-'Arabi uses this image of the two bodies of water, fresh and salty, as well as the *barzakh* (liminal interstice) between them to construct an entire cosmic vision where everything is a '*barzakh* between two *barzakhs*'.

But he is also returning this metaphor back inwardly towards the human being. In this regard, Ibn al-'Arabi is building upon the narration: "The sickness is within you and cure also within you. You assume yourself to be something small, when in reality the entire cosmos is folded within", attributed either to the Prophet ﷺ or his cousin Ali b. Abi Talib.

Here, Ibn al-'Arabi presents the *jism* (human body) as a symbol of the physical world and salty water, our *ruh* (spirit) as an allusion to the spiritual realm and fresh water while our *nafs* (soul) emerges as the *barzakh* between them.

More than that, the Andalusian mystic perceives the soul as a child born in the marriage between the body and spirit. In turn, as William Blake states, the universe can be a window into the human soul and vice versa.

Let us not also forget that for Ibn al-'Arabi Christ is an apt representation of this *barzakhiya* (liminality) of the soul as a child born in the proverbial marriage between the body, represented by Mary, and the holy spirit Gabriel. How is liminality important in your work? Do you find yourself thinking abundantly about the notion of the in-between?

"In reality, everything in existence is a *barzakh* between two things."

————

"When you are looking at two things, don't look at them, look between them."
-    John Baldessari

Continuing with our focus on the *barzakh* (liminality), I propose that this concept is perhaps the most relevant and revenant notion in Ibn al-'Arabi's teachings for our day and age.

I venture that every sense of liminality humanity is experiencing today, of being at the threshold of ethnic, religious, gender, sexual or any other identity is metaphysically rooted in this *barzakhiya*.

Let us remember that for Ibn al-'Arabi the human body, in all its eccentricities, fragilities and weaknesses is sacred and a window, as William Blake stated above, into the unknown. This window can be found, as John Baldessari mentions here, in the space between, at the *barzakh*.

As the days of our age progress, we come to find this metaphysical *barzakhiya*, our actual existential reality as an in-between, an imagination between *'adam* (nothingness) and *wujud* (everything), manifesting in a myriad of ways. The artist comes to remind humanity that its search is indeed sacred and its threads need to be weaved into a larger cosmic tapestry.

Here again, Ibn al-'Arabi, his contemporary interlocutors and the creative process teach us not to dismiss the physical form as traces of modernism proclaim through religious education today. Do you ever feel moved to expand the liminality from your work outwardly towards the world? What about the other way around? How does all of that manifest?

"The realm of imagination is one where spirits are corporealized and bodies are spiritualized."

"Where the spirit does not work with the hand, there is no art."
-    Leonardo Da Vinci

In this third conversation about imagination and the *barzakh*, Ibn al-ʿArabi brings these two concepts together to highlight that *ʿalam al-khayal* (realm of imagination), between the physical and spiritual realms, is also the *barzakh* (liminal interstice) between these two worlds.

In his foreword to Henry Corbin's *Alone With the Alone: Creative Imagination in the Sufism of Ibn ʿArabi*, Harold Bloom emphasizes that the realm of imagination is the land of dreams and creative inspiration, further highlighting the sacrality of art and creativity that we've discussed so far.

In this conversation, both Ibn al-ʿArabi and Leonardo Da Vinci reveal exactly how the creative process is sacred and what it entails: a paradoxical meeting between bodies and spirits. I say 'paradoxical' because as Ibn al-ʿArabi mentions, bodies are dense and bound by time and space whereas spirits are the opposite, subtle and free from our three dimensions.

This is precisely why the *barzakh* of imagination exists, to allow bodies to become more spiritualized and spirits to dress themselves in subtle forms and meet one another, just as the material *barzakh* allows fresh and salty waters to mingle without transgressing the boundaries of either body.

In other words, the entire premise of art and creativity is paradoxical, perplexing, contradictory and – hence – miraculous. It is nothing short of extraordinary that you as an artist are able to breathe the inexpressible through word, color or sound. How do you sense this birthing process in your work?

"Some knowledge is neither authenticated according to *naql* [transmitted sources] nor *'aql* [rational reflection], rather *kashf* [unveiling]."

———

"To become truly immortal, a work of art must escape all human limits: logic and commonsense will only interfere. But these barriers are broken, it will enter the realms of childhood visions and dreams."
-    Giorgio DeChirico

Ibn al-'Arabi mentions this specifically in the context of the *hadith* of the Hidden Treasure that we discussed in the previous chapter, which as we mentioned at the time is verified neither according to *naql* or *'aql* but only *kashf*, as the Andalusian mystic mentions here.

Giorgio DeChirico provides the apt framework for us to apply Ibn al-'Arabi's conversation here to the context of art and the creative process. This is especially poignant for us Muslim artists and the struggles we have finding our place and space in our community's religious discourse.

As mentioned beforehand, much of our contemporary religious education is largely a product of the enlightenment and a modernist prizing of the rational sciences that can be institutionalized, curriculumized and appropriated within the apparatus of industrialization. The essence of the creative process, to make connections where none seem possible or exist, does not fit into this paradigm. This is why artists are regarded as frivolous entertainers at most, not custodians of the faith, as they traditionally were and should continue to be.

Ibn al-'Arabi is here to sanctify the *kashf* of the artist, otherwise known as creative inspiration. As we saw previously, he also regards human – not only Muslim or believers – imagination as an extension of its Divine counterpart. As a Muslim artist, how do your creative inspirations and works fit into the dreams you have as well as your conversations with God?

"Love is the lover's longing for union with the beloved. If that union were to occur, then the object of love changes, from longing for the union to happen to its continuation. Thus, the object of love is never truly achieved. Rather, the object of love does not really exist."

———

"Have no fear of perfection, you will never achieve it."
- 	Salvadore Dali

This last quote by Ibn al-'Arabi in this chapter gives context to the struggle of the artist. What is the objective of art? Is it a specific work to complete? If not, what should the destination of the artist be in their work?

In *Art and Fear*, authors David Bayles and Ted Orland state that the biggest danger for the artist is not failure, but rather success. The fear of not only having no next project to look forward to, but also of not being able to surpass previous accomplishments can be detrimental to the artist.

This is where Ibn al-'Arabi's and Salvadore Dali's advices are pertinent, helpful and hopeful. In line with both of these two approaches, John Caputo remarks in *On Religion* that God is not the answer, but the opening of the question.

In this, as in many other aspects, art and faith are united. The objective of both journeys is not a particular reward or acknowledgment, even though that may be necessary often to alleviate doubts that artists have about their talents and callings.

The very struggle of the artist, to reach a particular end in sight, reveals a return to the beginning, as the Prophet ﷺ said in the aforementioned conversation: "Time has curved in its original form on the day that God created the heavens and earth", whence we learn to enjoy the journey for its own sake. How do you liberate yourself from attachments to particular works, successes or failures in your craft?

Chapter Three: *Saints and Scholars*

"The reason human beings love beautiful voices is because it reminds them of the day that God spoke to them." – Habib Umar b. Hafidh

————

"Did you know that the human voice is the only pure instrument? That it has notes no other instrument has? It is like being between the keys of a piano. The notes are there, you can sing them, but they cannot be found on any instrument. That is like me, I live in between this. I live in both worlds, the black and white world."
-   Nina Simone

Habib Umar b. Hafidh returns us here to our discussion on the primordial power of music, as the language of the spiritual realm and, as Ibn al-'Arabi explains, the original scripture. Habib Umar, however, provides a Qur'anic reference for this significance of sound.

In agreement with Habib Umar is the contemporary Muslim lady saint Hajjah Aminah Adil who describes in her prophetic biography, *Muhammad: The Messenger of Islam*, that in the primordial realm every human being interacted with the light of the Prophet ﷺ.

Those who saw his eyebrows were destined to become painters. Those who saw the palms of his hands became calligraphers, while those who saw his shadow became singers and musicians.

Incidentally, during his migration with the Prophet ﷺ, his confidant Abu Bakr remarked that he ﷺ does not have a shadow. So, what did singers and musicians exactly see in the primordial realm? A dimension of his reality that nobody else is able to witness. Perhaps, that is what music is trying to express as Nina Simone explains, where notes are there but cannot be found.

How do you feel your art is able to convey Divine or Prophetic realities that linger beyond the grasp of language?

"Listen to the reed-flute and how it laments its separation from the reed-bed." – Mevlana Rumi

———

"Sometimes the break in your heart is like the hole in the flute. Sometimes it is the place where the music comes through."
-    Andrea Gibson

This is not only the most well-known opening verse from *The Mathnavi*, but perhaps of all mystical poetry in the world today. Rumi situates the reed-flute, music and art generally not only within the spiritual journey but also the contemporary realities of diaspora, migration and exile.

This also returns us to our conversation on the in-between and *barzakh* with Ibn al-'Arabi, emphasizing the rootedness of all instances of liminality today in a higher spiritual vision. Meanwhile, Andrea Gibson provides a more intimate focus on the individual and the exile we might feel within.

All these themes have been explored beautifully by Alex Kronemer in his recent animated masterpiece *Lamya's Poem* about a young Syrian refugee who finds solace in *The Mathnavi* as she flees her native country and as Rumi's own words become a portal for Lamya to meet the poet in *'alam al-khayal* (imaginal realm).

Both Lamya and Rumi find themselves exiled due to war, and what unites them is the reed-flute, which was also separated from its home, the reed-bed. Then, it was burnt, broken, emptied from within and carved out. Only then is it able to channel the Divine Breath and produce music.

And so it is, that musical instruments are sages that teach us more than how to breathe beauty through sound, but also how to become musical instruments ourselves in Divine Hands. This is the 'art of living'. How does your art transcend the boundary of a craft and becomes a raft for the 'art of living' in your life?

"Art is all spirituality and spirituality is all art. You need taste to belong in a spiritual fraternity and to appreciate good art." – Shaykh Hisham Kabbani

---

"Art is born and takes hold wherever there is a timeless and insatiable longing for the spiritual."
- Andrei Tarkovsky

Shaykh Hisham Kabbani expresses here what I have long held to be true and set down as the vision in my previous book, *A Nostalgic Remembrance: Sufism and the Breath of Creativity*, namely that the creative process and mystical experience are mirrored movements.

Both journeys can be defined as 'making connections where none seem possible or exist' and 'translating the ineffable into the tangible'. But on more concrete social terms, I hold artists of all faiths today to be custodians of a conversation that resides at the heart of all the world's spiritual traditions.

Countless times have I heard non-Muslim artists express truths that are almost found verbatim in the writings of Ibn al-'Arabi. In those moments, I am reminded of a piece of wisdom that the contemporary Muslim thinker Sayyid Hossein Nasr told me, that "when people see a mountain, what attracts them is the peak. Only if the summit is captivating will they struggle to climb the base."

Saints of all crafts, including painting, music, poetry and religion, speak the same language, which we call the 'siren song at the summit.' And it is a remarkable moment in our history when non-Muslim artists can more eloquently express Islam's spiritual truths than the faith's own scholars and preachers.

How would you describe the spiritual dimensions of your craft in five themes or emotions that are not religiously technical in nature?

"Your desire for seclusion when God has placed you in the world is a hidden whim, while your desire to be in the world when He has placed you in seclusion is a fall from a lofty rank." – Ibn 'Ata' Allah al-Sikandari

———

"Creative work is a gift to the world and every being in it. Do not cheat us of your contribution. Give us what you have got."
-    Steven Pressfield

Among the many jewels that Ibn 'Ata' Allah al-Sikandari provides in his book of Aphorism, this one is an essential antidote for Muslim artists who were made to believe that publicizing their work and talent is a form of arrogance.

Alongside this, there is also a widespread sentiment among Muslim artists that they first need to 'ground themselves' before pursuing the creative path. To be honest, I am not sure what this means exactly? Are artists electric wires that need to be grounded or coffee beans that need to be made into fine powder?

In all seriousness, if by grounding we mean a sense of firm footedness in spirituality, then I believe the best toolset an artist can be given are confidence and conviction in the sacredness of their calling and craft, and to allow them the liberation to listen to God directly, not only through exegetical efforts by scholars past and present, speak to them through His Words.

Echoing Steven Pressfield's sentiment, I would further add that depriving the world of the beauty that you are able to channel is a betrayal of God's Gift, first and foremost. He is the One who granted you this talent, and no scholar can or should have the right to deprive you of pursuing this passion.

Rather, follow the Prophet ﷺ who said: "Seek council from your heart, even when they council you." How do you transition between seclusions and publicity in your craft?

"How many a sin that leaves behind brokenness is better than a good deed that leaves behind arrogance."
– Ibn 'Ata' Allah al-Sikandari

"Art consoles those who are broken by life."
-    Vincent Van Gogh

This quote, also from al-Sikandari's *Aphorisms*, sanctifies brokenness that resides at the heart of art and the creative process. Vincent Van Gogh, who experienced immense heartache in his life, expresses this truth eloquently.

Despite casual references of *tawba* (repentance) in sermons and lectures, the contemporary Muslim community does not fully appreciate brokenness. Rather, there is a dangerous idealism borrowed from the protestant ethic that prizes economic success to an obsessive degree and which has suffused itself within Islamic religiosity.

This appears in a mercantile engagement with God; a sense of expectation of reward as recompense for the worship that one does, despite the countless narrations in Qur'an and Hadith that emphasize the worthlessness of human effort when faced with Divine Grace and Judgment.

When it comes to sin or brokenness, there is often an outright shunning of mental illnesses, denial of domestic abuse against women by men in positions of power and what can only be described in today's terminology as 'gaslighting' of the sufferings and redemptive passions of the youth.

With no clear hope in sight that the community at large will change its course and discourse, it remains the sole task of Muslim artists to excavate the mercy inherent in our tradition from the Qur'an, Hadith and writings of Muslim saints like al-Sikandari in order to forge a new path forward, one of living creatively and creative living.

How do you find your art to be a medium for giving voice to the voiceless in the Muslim community and larger society?

"It has reached me that somebody made a candlestick statue for the king with a small figure of a man that emerges from inside the candlestick every hour of the night and greets the king. Then when the dawn prayer time comes, the statue emerges with an extended greeting to wake the king from his sleep. I was inspired to make a similar work with an extra statue of a lion that stands next to the man. The colors of the man's eyes and the lions also change every hour and correspond to the color of the candlestick that also fluctuates every hour."
– Imam al-Qarafi

"I saw the angel in the marble and carved until I set him free."
-    Michelangelo

This conversation with the Maliki scholar al-Qarafi is a remarkable introspection on scholarship and creativity. I chose this excerpt specifically due to the disparaging view on sculpture as an art form in the Muslim community.

Not only did al-Qarafi regard this craft as permissible but practiced it himself as a sculptor. In this anecdote, he is inspired by a gift that was given to the king and felt obliged to include his own artwork in a scholarly book on Islam.

This single fact is far more important than the permissibility of sculpture as a craft, which as I mentioned in the introduction is beneath the scope of this book. We, Muslim artists, are not at this juncture to legitimize our journey but to grow as Muslim artists among ourselves and the larger collective of creatives nationally and worldwide.

If al-Qarafi, a Maliki scholar, mentions his art in a book on scholarship, why should our art as Muslim artists not be regarded as a spiritual compendium? As an artist and scholar himself, al-Qarafi understood the sacredness of the creative process. Do you ever feel that your art can and should be considered as an interpretive lens of scripture?

**"I wish all of you would watch cinema once in your life. You would see that it has glimpses of spiritual reality."
– Shaykh Ibrahim Niass**

———

"The cinema has done more for my spiritual life than the church. My ideas of fame, success and beauty all originate from the big screen. Whereas Christian religion is retreating everywhere and losing more and more influence; film has filled the vacuum and supports us with myths and action-controlling images."
- John Updike

At around 2007, a turning point in my life, I underwent a crisis of faith after finding myself at a local mosque with a dry portrayal of Islam. At that crucial juncture, it was a television drama, *Lost*, that replenished my spiritual well.

The epiphany that occurred to me while watching this incredible production on spirituality, self-discovery, letting go and penitence is that in the years I have spent listening to sermons and lectures at my local mosque, never had I come across depth and meaningfulness as I found in one episode of *Lost*.

My own experience is one among many that is verified by Shaykh Ibrahim Niass and John Updike. They meet at this interstice and agreement about the spiritual potential in cinema precisely because saints like Shaykh Ibrahim Niass are artists of the soul, while artists like Updike are saints at heart.

What both Shaykh Ibrahim and Updike also highlight is the crucial role that art played in spirituality at one point in time. Whereas now art is seen as frivolous entertainment, and a distraction from more 'serious' religious pursuits like scholastic learning, in the past it was the sine qua non of spiritual expression and learning.

Have you ever received inspiration for your art from film or television?

"What colors cannot describe, words may explain. But that to which even words cannot allude, only music can express." – Hazrat Inayat Khan

———

"Music expresses that which cannot be said and on which it is impossible to be silent."
-   Victor Hugo

Hazrat Inayat Khan, founder of the Inayatia Sufi order, embodies the convergence of art and spirituality in his life and teachings. Originally a sitar musician from India, he later joined the Chishti Sufi order and was sent by his guide as a representative to America to spread Sufism, specifically through music.

In his groundbreaking work, *The Mysticism of Sound and Music*, Hazrat Inayat Khan outlines a vision of a musical universe, one where the alternation of night and day, our heartbeats, change of seasons and every fluctuation and repetition in the cosmic symphony demonstrates that ours is a musical existence.

I use this emphasis on the rhythmic movements stirring our universe to also deduce that, given that all are God's Words as the Qur'an states regarding Jesus and which Ibn al-'Arabi extends to every created thing, this universe is a versification of Divine Speech.

Rather, God speaks only poetry, not prose. For if our existence was 'prosaic', there would be no rhythm, no constancy or reference to the chaos of change that we experience. This rhyme that is manifest in all created beings behooves us to think and feel through a Divine Poiesis.

Therefore, as Hazrat Inayat Khan explains, music is that primordial art form that expresses what resides beyond the language of ink and dye. Victor Hugo adds that what music breathes, despite being inexpressible, must nevertheless be birthed. In this way, music is a reminder and remembrance of lost memories. How would you describe your craft in music or what are its musical dimensions?

"The fifth symphony of Beethoven is entirely about God and faith." – Shaykh Ali Goma

———

"Music is a higher revelation than all wisdom and
philosophy."
- Ludwig van Beethoven

Beethoven's compositions have often been used as examples of Divinely Inspired music. And yet, what is more significant is this musician's own position on the Divine Origin of music; a stance that inspires his fifth symphony, which Shaykh Ali Goma praised, and all his other works.

Returning to *Art and Fear*, the authors clarify a poignant distinction between an artwork and the creative process of the artist: "Whereas the general audience is interested in the work, those who are artists themselves are invested in the process that produced it."

To this I add that if an artwork is the body, then the creative process of the artist is its spirit. Where we as a collective of Muslim artists in the West need to reach is to transition from discussing the body of our art to conversing about its spirit.

I am often left speechless at the depth of reflections by non-Muslim artists on various channels, such as *Art21* and *Louisiana Channel*, where painters, sculptors, photographers and architects will talk about themes like witnessing, death and rebirth, emotional intensity and various other topics.

This spirit of art, the creative process, is an important conversation for Muslim artists specifically to have because that is the *barzakh* at which spirituality meets creativity. It is at this juncture that the Qur'an, Hadith and writings of saints like Ibn al-'Arabi can help us, not only in our own crafts, but also to converse with the larger collective of artists. How often do you reflect on the relationship between your creative process and the works that it births and breathes?

"Sacred knowledge, if you give it some of yourself, it will give you nothing. If you give it all of yourself, will give you something." – Imam al-Shafi'i

---

"Music is a spiritual thing. You don't play with music If you play with music, you will die young. You see, because when the higher forces give you the gift of music, it must be well used for the gift of humanity."
- 　Fela Kuti

When I first came across Sir Michael Caine's advice on approaching acting as merely a fulltime job, as opposed to a way of life, I immediately thought of this statement by Imam al-Shafi'i. Acting is, as are all the arts, a sacred craft. Reaching the summit of mastery in this and other vocations delivers one to the shore of sainthood in that particular art form.

Saints of all crafts, as we mentioned earlier, speak the same language, that 'siren song at the summit'. To reach that peak however, per Imam al-Shafi'i's and Fela Kuti's advice, one must first take seriously the sacredness of the Divine Gift entrusted to them.

I experience this myself everyday with the Oud and Arabic music. There is an Arab proverb that says: "One day for us, another against us." In music specifically and art generally, it is more like "one day for us and ten against us." Or as my Oud teacher Tariq al-Jundi expressed: "You need to put your heart and gallbladder in a freezer if you want to master the Oud."

In turn, art is the most sacred of knowledges for the one in whose heart it has been planted as a Divine Gift. The difficulty we experience in cultivating and growing in this calling is not meaningless.

Rather, nothing meaningful can come easily. The architect Peter Cook who insists on drawing blueprints by hand explains: "The time it takes my hand to learn how to draw something is enough time for my mind and heart to understand it as well." Have you ever experienced your craft as sacred knowledge, to which you comfortably and ecstatically give your entirety?

**A religious scholar during the time of the Muslim saint
'Abdul Ghani al-Nabulusi had heard that the saint was
playing musical instruments in his lodge. He went to
reprimand the saint. When he entered the lodge, he
found *saz* hanging all around the walls of the lodge. He
began scolding al-Nabulusi, at which point the saint
simply pointed with his finger at all the instruments,
each of which began to declare the *shahada*: *la ilāha illa
Allah* (there is no god but God).**

"Tones sound and roar and storm about me until I have set
them down in notes."
-     Ludwig van Beethoven

The Damascene saint Abdul Ghani al-Nabulusi is a well known
student in the school of Ibn al-'Arabi. In this conversation, he
shows just how much he has inherited from the latter in his
appreciation of music and the arts.

What this anecdote shows most importantly is the constant
struggle between saints and those whom Ibn al-'Arabi and
Imam Ghazali label as *'ulama al-rusum* (scholars of outer form)
who not only separate *sharia* (law) from *haqiqa* (reality), but
have altogether neglected the metaphysical underpinnings of
our existence, thereby turning the law, faith and all of life into
a mere shell of its true potential.

It should not be surprising that Beethoven is more in agreement with al-Nabulusi and witnesses what he experienced of the reality of music than the Muslim scholar who sought to disparage the saint for his love of musical instruments.

Note – pun intended – that the terms 'tone' and 'note' are anagrams, mere permutations of one another. In other words, a tone is always waiting to be reborn as a note at the hands of a musician. Whereas saints of their crafts like Beethoven and al-Nabulusi see both the spirit of the tone and body of the note, 'scholars of outer form', in every age, perceive only the body.

Have you every heard your craft's instruments speak to you? What language do they communicate and what knowledge do they convey to you?

"Beloveds of my heart, drink *al-qahwa al-qarqafiya* [cold and creamy coffee]. Indeed, if any of you drink it, they will not go to sleep save that springs of wisdom will flow forth from their heart." – Shaykh Ibrahim al-Dusuqi

———

"Coffee is not to be tasted in a hurry. Coffee is the sister of time and should be tasted slowly. Coffee is the sound of taste and fragrance. Coffee is a contemplation and deep journey into the soul and memories."
- Mahmoud Darwish

Coffee has been the companion of artists, especially in our day and age, since what seems like eternity – contradiction intended. While the famous Egyptian saint Shaykh Ibrahim al-Dusuqi shows that coffee is spiritually potent, the Palestinian poet Mahmoud Darwish brings out its importance also as a marker of memories and maker of memoirs for artists.

Of course, as we have been emphasizing thus far, the spiritual and creative allusions are hardly exclusive but rather mirror one another. Darwish dedicated countless poems to coffee and coffee shops, revealing its place as the proverbial ink with which he forged the contours of his artistry.

I bring both these visions together, al-Dusuqi's and Darwish's, to say that as artists we must pay attention to the behavioral eccentricities we develop around our craft. What you like to wear, say, smell like or drink while working at your art, including the organization of your studio or lack thereof, is hardly haphazard.

Do not be scared to regard it as sacred. Ibn al-'Arabi remarks that each saint receives Divine Inspiration through a physical sense or behavior. Some laugh, others cry, sneeze or twitch. It is a contagious mannerism that overflows its grace to all in their presence.

What are some of your eccentric sacred rituals when you work on your craft?

**"Whosever knowledge increases, their criticism
decreases." – Imam Abdullah b. Alawi al-Haddad**

————

"The artist is the only one qualified to criticize his art,
because only the artist knows what he was trying to express
and how satisfied he is with the attempt."
-    Ron Brackin

This poignant teaching by the Hadhrami saint Imam Abdullah
b. Alawi al-Haddad, I feel, is a crucial advice for artists
specifically, and the Muslim community generally, in how we
approach collective art and culture.

By its very nature, the enterprise of art critique, whether in the
written, visual, auditory or moving arts requires a certain
amount of binding and limiting the work at hand to specific
categories. It is truly not a facetious question to ask: what
makes a work of art good or bad?

Whatever criterion we might use to judge a poem, novel,
painting or musical composition necessarily carves out from
the work those aspects or dimensions that do not fit its
standards of beauty and perfection. Even if the critic tries to
approach art objectively, remarking that they try their best to
consider the work on its own merit, they will still bring their

own experience as a lens through which to appreciate beauty in word and world.

As a student of Ibn al-'Arabi's teachings, I do not believe there is a way to escape from the subjective prism that shapes our engagement with art. However, what we can do is to approach it not as speakers, but listeners who silently await the artist to speak from within the work.

This Ibn al-'Arabi describes as our relationship with God, either as *muhaddith* (speaker) or *muhaddath* (spoken to). If we wish to speak to Him, He is attentive to us. But if we wish to hear His Response, we must be silent and listen. What is your opinion on critique as pertaining to your craft and art generally?

When Abdullah b. Abu Bakr al-Aydarus, the son of Abu Bakr al-Aydarus wanted to call people to God, his father asked him to go to the marketplace and find somebody who is worse than him.

He first came across a drunkard Muslim and thought that he was better than this sinner, but then realized that he could die in a worse state than him. Then, he came across a disbeliever and likewise thought he could die in a worse state than him.

Lastly, he came across a dog and thought: "The dog will turn to dust on the Day of Judgment but I might enter hell. So, the dog might be better than me." Upon returning to his father and telling him what transpired, his father said: "Now you can call people to God."

———

"I retain, but suspend, my personal taste to deal with the panoply of the art I see. I have a trick for doing justice to an uncongenial work: 'What would I like about this if I liked it?' I may come around; I may not. Failing that, I wonder, what must the people who like this be like?"
- Peter Schjeldahl

Continuing with our focus on art critique from the previous conversation, Habib Abdullah b. Abu Bakr al-Aydarus, also from Yemen, is taught by his father Habib Abu Bakr al-Aydarus a lesson on criticism that harmonizes with art critic Peter Schjeldahl's advice: to turn our observation of art and world inwardly.

This is the quintessential mirroring between inner word and outer world that Ibn al-'Arabi taught us previously. By perceiving every human being and animal as better than him, al-Aydarus was essentially receiving creation as the Creator loves them. And this is the same introspective lens that Schjeldahl uses to approach art, to imagine what those who like a work actually enjoy of it.

I add to this the important question: beyond any fallacies or faults that we deem are crippling in a work, can we find its artist's initial sacred gaze into Divine Imagination? What are they trying to say?

What strategies do you use to enjoy a work of art that does not appeal to you at first glance?

While listening to music, a man approached Mevlana Rumi and said to him: "When I hear this music, I can see the gates of paradise closing." Rumi responded to him: "They might be closing for you but are opening for us."

———

"Music is God's Gift to man, the only art of heaven given to earth and the only art of earth we take to heaven."
-     Walter Savage Landor

I use the opportunity of this conversation to reiterate a previous point: as Muslim artists, our creative community does not have to be our coreligionists, but those among them and outside the Muslim congregation who not only appreciate the arts and culture but more importantly are able to appreciate the depth of conversing about the creative process, the spirit of art.

A study done recently on Muslim students in Islamic schools across the United States revealed that the most common word in their vocabulary is 'obligatory'. This shows that the entire epistemology of our community of faith has become – as I mentioned previously – binary; a digital division between 0's *haram* and 1's *halal.*

When our entire prism of approaching society and culture are categories and definitions, then we are no longer able to enjoy film, music, novels or a casual visit to the museum. This is because the arts, as the building blocks of culture, by their very design cultivate contradiction and focus on the gray areas in our morality.

Considering all of this, it is important for us Muslim artists to transition from binary conversations that obsess over clearly defined boundaries and linger instead on the ambiguous margins where music might be heaven closing for some yet, at the same time, opening for others. What is the importance of ambivalence and ambiguity in your craft?

Ibn Kurr, a Hanbali scholar, once passed by singers and was able to move his mule in a way such that it began dancing according to the rhythm of their music.

———

"My music is best understood by children and animals."
-    Igor Stravinsky

Like the Maliki scholar Imam al-Qarafi, the Hanbali scholar Ibn Kurr was also well versed in the arts, specifically music. It seems to have been a particular tradition in Madinah that many scholars were singers and musicians, alongside whatever science of religion they sought to specialize in.

However, unlike the contemporary Muslim approach to art that regards it at most as a hobby or frivolous pastime, al-Qarafi and Ibn Kurr show us that, in the past, it was inseparable from their spiritual and religious vocations.

Ibn Kurr specifically seems to understand better than many of his coreligionists today that enjoying music is a disposition inherent in all of God's Creation, even animals. Rather, the inability to enjoy music – and by extension all art – is a sign of a deviation from the norm.

Also, both Ibn Kurr and musician Igor Stravinsky return us to a conversation with the Prophet ﷺ that we discussed in the first chapter, regarding rainfall as a *hadith* (recent arrival from God). Animals and children are also, like rainfall, recent arrivals from the Divine Presence.

They are, in the truest sense, *ummi* (unschooled), unfettered by the veils of rational knowledge and can still hear the primordial Divine Address. How do you try to remain or return to a state of *ummiyya* (primordial child-like nature) through your work and craft?

Ibrahim b. Sa'd al-Zuhri, a prominent scholar of Hadith from Madina, was known for not only permitting singing but practicing the art himself. Somebody came to seek narrations of hadith from him and heard him singing. He said to al-Zuhri: "I was so eager to receive hadith from you, but now I will make sure to never do so." Al-Zuhri said: "Good riddance, I swear by God I will never narrate hadith in Baghdad save that I will sing beforehand."

––––––

"My music is the spiritual expression of what I am, my faith, knowledge and being."
-    John Coltrane

Ibrahim b. Sa'd al-Zuhri, another scholar from Madina, extends his sacred appreciation of the arts beyond Ibn Kurr and al-Qarafi. He associated his love for singing with the transmission of hadith. And he only became more adamant about this connection when criticized by someone from *'ulama al-rusum* (scholars of outer form) that we mentioned before.

This anecdote continues wherein the Muslim ruler at the time had heard of this exchange and called al-Zuhri to his court. He asked him to narrate a particular hadith. Al-Zuhri requested an Oud to play. The caliph smiled and understood how important music was for this scholar.

This is precisely what the saint of Jazz John Coltrane expresses, that 'his music is the spiritual expression of what he is, his faith, knowledge and being'. And now, beginning from Coltrane's statement, I would like us to return to al-Zuhri's passion for hadith and music.

Whereas many in the Muslim community today will perceive music and hadith as two separate vocations, the first definitively of lower rank than the second, I do not hold that to be true. I believe that al-Zuhri insisted on singing and playing the Oud prior to reciting hadith because he is convinced that the breath of revelation imminent in the Prophet's ﷺ speech overflowed its meanings to music, whence both languages shared its meanings. Do you associate your craft with any spiritual rituals of your faith?

Ismail b. Jami' al-Qurashi was a prominent scholar who accompanied imam Malik. He studied Qur'an and Hadith, then became a singer and surpassed all others during his lifetime in this craft.

———

"I play the notes as they are written, but it is God who makes the music."
-    Johann Sebastian Bach

Ismail al-Qurashi continues the conversation with al-Zuhri and John Coltrane, revealing the extent to which, on the one hand, music can be a spiritual practice and, on the other, faith — necessarily – a creative endeavor. However, whereas Ibn Kurr and al-Zuhri practiced both the religious craft of hadith transmission and music, al-Qurashi seems to have altogether left the former vocation in favor of the arts.

It is remarkable that so many of the anecdotes in this chapter echo struggles many Muslim artists experience today. In Egypt, my mother's country of birth and my own spring of musical inspiration, musicians who wanted to master the art of *maqamat* (modalities of Arabic music) traditionally began with Qur'an recitation.

Reciters during the first half of the 20th century, known as the Golden Age of Arabic Music, like Mustafa Ismail were celebrated as the standard in musicality and mastery of *maqamat*, despite never studying the art formally. The first lady of Arabic music, Umm Kulthum, herself began as a Qur'an reciter, which granted her the ability to sing lyrics in classical Arabic impeccably.

The contemporary Muslim community believes that there is only one proper way to approach, benefit and engage with scripture, hadith and the wider teachings of Islam. In truth, however, every craft and vocation has its own Divine Well and vision of scripture, whence: "Every people have come to know their drinking place" (2:60).

How do you feel that your craft and art shapes your engagement with scripture and Islam at large?

Al-Fayruzabadi was a prominent Sufi and scholar of Hadith. He also memorized biographies of many pious saints and their poems and used to listen to music and dance. He also had the peculiar habit of informing everyone he met that he would pray for them specifically while dancing and listening to music.

————

"Prayer is the song of the heart. It reaches the ear of God even if it is mingled with the cry and tumult of a thousand men."
- Khalil Gibran

Each of these anecdotes takes us deeper into the sanctity of music, as perceived by past Muslim scholars. Al-Fayruzabadi not only enjoyed music and singing but perceived the time of *sama'* (audition) as a *sa'at istijaba* (time when prayers and supplications are answered).

What Fayruzabadi reveals here is what Shahab Ahmed describes in *What is Islam? The Importance of Being Islamic*, that Islam is not a system of rituals and beliefs, but rather a 'process of making meaning'. Each instance of time, events, people, actions and the artifacts of the sacred can – and should – be considered an archetype that can dress itself in a myriad of forms.

In turn, *sa'at al-istijaba* (the hour when prayers and supplications are answered by God) designated in Islam at specific intervals (e.g., last third of the night, holy occasions) are extended by al-Fayruzabadi to include the time of musical audition. Why? Because for him, music is his sacred space that necessarily has its own *wudu* (ablution), *salat* (prayer), *zakat* (alms) and *hajj* (pilgrimage), to mention a few.

Undoubtedly, many *'ulama al-rusum* (scholars of outer form) did and will misunderstand al-Fayruzabadi's habit, but we see again that it is artists like Khalil Gibran who truly understand the spirit beyond the form; for just as music is prayer, so must prayer be innocent like music. Do you feel that the time when you produce or consume art is a *sa'at istijaba* (hour of answered prayers)?

Aamir b. Saad narrated that he entered upon Qarza b. Kaab and Abu Masud during a wedding while some young girls were singing. He said to them: "This is happening in your house oh companions of the prophet ﷺ?" They said: "Sit down if you want and listen with us or get out. We have permission to enjoy ourselves during weddings."

"Music was my refuge. I could crawl into the space between the notes and curl my back to loneliness."
- Maya Angelou

We find many such anecdotes from the lives of the Prophet's ﷺ companions, that they were somewhat blunt in their response to others, even other companions, who sought to criticize them in favor of religious strictures.

Returning to the Prophet's poet Hassan b. Thabit whom we discussed in the first chapter. While reciting poetry in the mosque one day, presumably after the Prophet's ﷺ passing, Umar tried to stop him, to which Hassan responded: "I used to read my poetry here when someone who is much better than you listened to me."

Between Hassan, Qarza and Abu Mas'ud there is no room for fanaticism in Islam. You simply cannot establish a civilization by censuring art. This is a pivotal point which many Muslims today do not understand, even those who merely entertain the idea that music and other art forms are impermissible.

But as countless Muslim scholars and John Coltrane have informed us, and Maya Angelou does here as well, music is not simply a form of entertainment during weddings, but the very expression of one's faith and being.

Let us be unequivocal about this: as Muslim artists, art is our private intimate time with God and worship of Him. This just as *salat* is the universal public ritual that we share with other Muslims. How does your art help you paradoxically set boundaries to keep expansiveness within and constriction without?

"Divine sound is the cause of all manifestation. The knower of the mystery of sound knows the mystery of the whole universe." – Hazrat Inayat Khan

———

"Music is the Divine Way to tell beautiful, poetic things to the heart."
- Pablo Casals

In our second to last conversation in this book, we return to Hazrat Inayat Khan for one more insight into the sacredness of sound and music. But this time, I would like to linger at a different frontier, contemplating in an Akbarian fashion the metaphysical threads weaved by etymology.

The word 'sound' in English is a homonym that refers both to 'sonic vibrations' and 'in good condition'. Meanwhile, 'music' is rooted in the 'muses', or the spirits that convey creative inspiration, as explained in writings of Greek philosophers.

But also in Islamic metaphysics, as Ibn al-'Arabi explains, sound is the first movement from God towards His Creation, through the imperative utterance: "Kun [Be!]" Ibn al-'Arabi mentions this while discussing the sacrality of *sama'* (audition) and music.

In complete agreement with Hazrat Inayat Khan, Ibn al-'Arabi roots human music back in its Divine Origin. Here, we have an interesting exchange: just our initial primordial engagement with the Creator was through listening and sound, so does He also await to hear back from us a reenactment of this performance.

This is the essence of the previous conversation with the Prophet ﷺ wherein he said: "God listens more attentively to the reciter with a beautiful voice than one of you listens to their musical instrument." Did you ever hear the primordial creative command *kun* in your work? And if so, did you ever seek to echo it back to the Source?

Once, while reciting the Qur'an, Imam Ja'far al-Sadiq kept repeating a verse until he fainted. When he awoke and was asked about the reason for fainting, he said: "I kept repeating the verse until I heard it from the One who spoke it."

"I am hearing music all the time. Yes, even now."
-    Miles Davis

This concluding conversation brings together many threads that we weaved together in the previous pages, with the hope of presenting a tapestry of sacrality and meaningfulness that can help us Muslim artists in our horizontal journey in society, vertical ascension towards God and the meeting between them at the *barzakh*.

If, as we have shown, sound and audition is the primordial and first meeting between Creator and creation, then as Ibn al-'Arabi emphasizes the utterance of the creative command must be continuous and incessant. Moreover, it is not really repeated since there can be no repetition in God's Creativity because that entails finitude whereas He is the Infinite.

Rather, we are all still experiencing the first spark of *kun*. It is still taking place, in a single moment beyond time and space. This solitary blink in Divine Time has ushered in all the rhythm, rhyme and links in our existence. All our art is but a remembrance that seeks to reignite the memory of what we are already experiencing.

To reach the saintly status of Imam Ja'far al-Sadiq, who pierced with every repetition of a verse from scripture the heavens of meaning until he reached that primordial sound, one must be 'continuously in prayer', as we mentioned in a previous conversation.

When such is you witness of art, as the saint of his craft Miles Davis shows, you cannot help but perform in spirit when your body is at rest. Rather, you become a performance in silence. Did you ever pierce the layers of your work to reach a primordial conversation between yourself and God, as He creates through you?